NEW DIRECTIONS FOR COMMUNITY COLLEGES

Arthur M. Cohen
EDITOR-IN-CHIEF

Florence B. Brawer
ASSOCIATE EDITOR

# Understanding the Impact of Reverse Transfer Students on Community Colleges

Barbara K. Townsend
*University of Missouri–Columbia*

EDITOR

Number 106, Summer 1999

JOSSEY-BASS PUBLISHERS
San Francisco

# ERIC®
## Clearinghouse for Community Colleges

UNDERSTANDING THE IMPACT OF REVERSE TRANSFER STUDENTS ON
COMMUNITY COLLEGES
Barbara K. Townsend
New Directions for Community Colleges, no. 106
Volume XXVII, number 2
Arthur M. Cohen, Editor-in-Chief
Florence B. Brawer, Associate Editor

New Directions for Community Colleges is indexed in Current Index to
Journals in Education (ERIC).

Microfilm copies of issues and articles are available in 16mm and 35mm,
as well as microfiche in 105mm, through University Microfilms Inc., 300
North Zeeb Road, Ann Arbor, Michigan 48106–1346.

ISSN 0194-3081          ISBN 0-7879-4847-0

NEW DIRECTIONS FOR COMMUNITY COLLEGES is part of The Jossey-Bass
Higher and Adult Education Series and is published quarterly by Jossey-
Bass Inc., Publishers, 350 Sansome Street, San Francisco, California
94104–1342, in association with the ERIC Clearinghouse for Community
Colleges. Periodicals postage paid at San Francisco, California, and at
additional mailing offices. POSTMASTER: Send address changes to New
Directions for Community Colleges, Jossey-Bass Inc., Publishers, 350 San-
some Street, San Francisco, California 94104–1342.

SUBSCRIPTIONS cost $60.00 for individuals and $107.00 for institutions,
agencies, and libraries. Prices subject to change.

THE MATERIAL in this publication is based on work sponsored wholly or
in part by the Office of Educational Research and Improvement, U.S.
Department of Education, under contract number RI-93-00-2003. Its con-
tents do not necessarily reflect the views of the Department or any other
agency of the U.S. Government.

EDITORIAL CORRESPONDENCE should be sent to the Editor-in-Chief, Arthur
M. Cohen, at the ERIC Clearinghouse for Community Colleges, University of California, 3051 Moore Hall, Box 951521, Los Angeles, California
90095–1521. All manuscripts receive anonymous reviews by external ref-
erees.

Cover photograph © Rene Sheret, After Image, Los Angeles, California,
1990.

www.josseybass.com

Printed in the United States of America on acid-free recycled paper con-
taining 100 percent recovered waste paper, of which at least 20 percent is
postconsumer waste.

7/878

# CONTENTS

# EDITOR'S NOTES

Traditional views of college enrollment and retention assume two paths to the baccalaureate. The more traditional one, in which students receive their degree from the four-year college at which they began as freshmen, underlies most four-year colleges' retention efforts, as well as many educational policymakers' understanding of college attendance. The other path is vertical transfer, in which a student transfers to a four-year school after completing a two-year associate degree.

In reality, only one out of three students graduates from the college where he or she started (Tinto, 1987). This phenomenon occurs partly because of the vertical transfer pattern. The vertical model of transfer, assumed by many policymakers to be the primary transfer function of two-year colleges, underlies the emphasis on two-year colleges' transfer rates.

Transfer studies conducted over the past few decades demonstrate the inadequacy of these two enrollment and retention models. Many students actually attend a variety of colleges in their path toward a degree, sometimes attending two schools simultaneously. Institutional attendance patterns may include starting at a two-year college, transferring laterally to another two-year school, and then vertically transferring to the four-year school from which they finally graduate. Another pattern is for a student to start at a four-year college, transfer to a two-year school, and then transfer again to a second and even a third four-year college before completing the baccalaureate. In yet another pattern, a student may begin at a two-year college, transfer to one four-year school and then transfer to another four-year school. Occasionally, students transfer among three or more four-year colleges (Kearney, Townsend, and Kearney, 1995).

This issue addresses a pattern that is emerging in importance for the two-year college: the pattern whereby students matriculate at a four-year college and transfer to a two-year school. Often labeled *reverse transfer students,* these students can be placed into two groups: (1) undergraduate students, who start their undergraduate education at a four-year school and then transfer to a two-year school, and (2) postbaccalaureate students, who complete a bachelor's degree or higher and then enroll at a two-year college. Students in this second group have been considered reverse transfers because at many, perhaps all, two-year colleges they can transfer in credits from their baccalaureate degree toward a certificate or an associate degree.

Administrators and faculty at two-year colleges have been aware of both types of reverse transfers since at least the 1960s. However, the presence of postbaccalaureate reverse transfers has recently been attracting national attention in other educational circles. For example, a 1997 *Chronicle of Higher Education* article bore the headline, "A Community College in Virginia Attracts Ph.D.'s—as Students" (Gose, p. A33). According to the article, "10 to 20 per cent of students at community colleges have at least a bachelor's degree" (p. A34).

The recruitment of reverse transfer students is a market niche for many two-year colleges, depending on their geographical location and nearness to universities. This issue explores the presence of reverse transfers and their impact on two-year colleges by presenting both previous research (Chapters One, Four, Five, and Seven) and research conducted for this issue (Chapters Two, Three, and Six).

In Chapter One, Barbara K. Townsend and John T. Dever describe the phenomenon of reverse transfer students by reviewing previous studies conducted at the institutional, district, state, and national levels. How enrollment of these students fits within the mission of the community college is also discussed.

The next three chapters focus entirely or primarily on reverse transfer students' reasons for attending community colleges. Chapter Two, written by Linda Serra Hagedorn and Consuelo Rey Castro, focuses on both undergraduate reverse transfers and postbaccalaureate reverse transfer students. The authors first detail enrollment patterns on a statewide level, particularly as they have been affected by California's decision to increase fees at its two-year schools, and then present interview results indicating why students have sought to attend the community college.

Next, James L. Catanzaro speaks from the perspective of a two-year college president when he writes in Chapter Three about recruiting reverse transfer students. Catanzaro profiles the different types of reverse transfers, the ways his institution (Chattanooga State Technical Community College in Tennessee) has recruited each type, and his reasons for encouraging their enrollment.

In Chapter Four, John W. Quinley and Melissa P. Quinley present a typology of postbaccalaureate reverse transfer students' motivations for attending two-year schools. The chapter draws on the results of interviews with forty postbaccalaureate reverse transfers in North Carolina.

The next three chapters focus primarily on reverse transfer students' behavior and their enrollment patterns while at a community college. Chapter Five, written by Susan K. Bach, Melissa A. Banks, David K. Blanchard, Mary K. Kinnick, Mary F. Ricks, and Juliette M. Stoering, examines the enrollment patterns of undergraduate students who began at Portland State University and then transferred to one or more of three two-year colleges in the area before transferring back to the university.

Chapter Six, by Terry L. Barnes and Laura M. Robinson, examines what reverse transfer students are like in Missouri. Included are the results of a survey of the chief academic officers of Missouri's twelve community college districts regarding their perceptions of this phenomenon.

In Chapter Seven, Barbara K. Townsend and Rivkah Y. Lambert draw from case studies they conducted separately to provide profiles of bachelor's-degree students at a technical institute in Tennessee and two community colleges in Maryland. Based on the results of student interviews, the authors indicate student behaviors that are both beneficial and potentially problematic for two-year colleges.

In Chapter Eight, Daniel J. Phelan discusses implications at both the institutional and external policymaking levels, given the growing presence of both types of reverse transfer students.

Chapter Nine, by Christine M. LeBard, provides a look at additional sources of information about reverse transfer students.

These chapters demonstrate that reverse transfer students contradict the traditional models of transfer on which so many retention studies have been based. Rather, these students' transfer behavior suggests a new model—one in which students switch from college to college, much the way television viewers switch channels. As long as a college serves students' purposes, they will stay, but once it no longer meets their needs, they will switch to another college. Perhaps they experience some temporary disconnect in attendance as they move from college to college, but they are ultimately in charge of their educational experience as they seek to achieve their educational goals.

Awareness of the growing presence of these self-directed students may serve as a catalyst for innovative state-level discussions about the missions of two-year colleges vis-à-vis those of four-year colleges. Policymakers, especially legislators, need to realize that serving undergraduate reverse transfers adds a new dimension to the two-year college's transfer function: that of receiving transfers from four-year schools. The growing presence of postbaccalaureate reverse transfers at two-year colleges also highlights the attraction of the community college to all classes and types of students.

Leaders of four-year colleges might see the reverse transfer pattern as a wake-up call regarding the nature of undergraduate students' experience at the four-year college and the value of the four-year degree in the job market, in the case of postbaccalaureate reverse transfers. Leaders of two-year colleges will be better able to understand the impact of reverse transfers on their colleges. Certainly, two-year college leaders, faced with insufficient state funding and high demand for student seats in competitive programs, will need to address the implications of reverse transfer students on their original mission of serving students not served by other institutions. Additionally, both two-year and four-year college leaders need to be cognizant that reverse transfers' switching back and forth among institutions is not fully understood by the general public nor by state policymakers. These students, especially "summer sessioners," may be counted as dropouts in state counts of enrollment, thus potentially affecting institutional funding and accountability measures.

Knowledge of reverse transfers may also lead to rethinking the motivations for student transfer, so that undergraduate students who leave an institution are no longer pejoratively viewed as dropouts but rather as students who know what they need and know where to get it. In addition, those who study student retention and enrollment patterns will better understand the complexity of these patterns and perhaps rethink models of undergraduate college choice.

## References

Gose, B. "A Community College in Virginia Attracts Ph.D.'s—as Students." *Chronicle of Higher Education,* July 11, 1997, pp. A33–34.

Kearney, G. W., Townsend, B. K., and Kearney, T. J. "Multiple-Transfer Students in a Public Urban University: Background Characteristics and Interinstitutional Movements. *Research in Higher Education,* 1995, *36* (3), 323–344.

Tinto, V. *Leaving College: Rethinking the Causes and Cures of Student Attrition.* Chicago: University of Chicago Press, 1987.

BARBARA K. TOWNSEND *is professor of higher education at the University of Missouri–Columbia. While a professor at the University of Memphis, she worked in the Office of Academic Affairs on transfer and articulation issues. She is a former community college faculty member and administrator.*

*Studies of reverse transfer students are reviewed, producing a profile of these students and their experiences in the two-year college.*

# What Do We Know About Reverse Transfer Students?

*Barbara K. Townsend, John T. Dever*

The mechanistic image of a pipeline that channels college-bound students directly from high school graduation to college entrance to baccalaureate attainment captures the traditional view of undergraduate college attendance. When the two-year college is considered part of the pipeline, it is only as a facilitator of the vertical flow from high school to college graduation. However, a far more realistic image of current college attendance patterns is suggested by the phrase "transfer swirl" (de los Santos and Wright, 1990). Subject to various currents in their lives, some students move from school to school like leaves twisting in the wind. They may swirl upward from a two-year to a four-year school, float laterally from one two-year school to another two-year school, or spin downward from a four-year to a two-year school.

In this chapter we will look at students who move from a four-year college to a two-year college. Called *reverse transfer students* because they transfer in a pattern that is the reverse of the traditional pipeline pattern, they are a growing presence within the two-year college. We will categorize these students, review what is known about their numbers, summarize studies that describe the students and their experiences in the two-year college, and discuss institutional rationales for admitting them.

## Categories of Reverse Transfer Students

The phrase "reverse transfer students" fails to capture the variations within this category of two-year students; they come in different types. The two most common are *undergraduate reverse transfer students* (URTSs) and *postbaccalaureate reverse transfer students* (PRTSs)—students who already have at least a bachelor's degree before they enroll at a two-year college.

Among URTSs are two subsets: (1) students who begin their education at a four-year school and then transfer to a two-year school and stay there for a while, perhaps to degree completion (the more common subset and the one that is typically meant by the term) and (2) temporary reverse transfers—students who attend a two-year college, often during the summer, simply to earn a few credits that can be transferred back to their four-year college. In Chapter Two, Hagedorn and Castro refer to these students as summer sessioners. Studies examining undergraduate reverse transfers typically fail to differentiate between summer sessioners and students who attend during the regular academic year.

The other primary group—PRTSs—may attend the two-year school for personal development, exploration of new career fields, or advancement within their current field (Kajstura and Keim, 1992). They are considered transfer students because at some two-year schools they can transfer in credits from their baccalaureate degree toward a degree. How many two-year colleges permit this reverse transfer of credits is unknown, but it appears that four-year credits are generally accepted unless they are outside a college's statute of limitations for courses in particular majors such as nursing.

Whereas research in the 1970s and 1980s focused more on URTSs, attention in the 1990s has shifted to PRTSs. In each instance, data have revealed something not anticipated when community colleges are conceived to function as a designated segment of an educational pipeline that flows in a single direction: community colleges are assuming multiple educational roles. In fact, the study of reverse transfers is integrally connected with the larger story of how community colleges in the past three decades have assumed a more comprehensive role, not just in higher education but in economic development and social opportunity.

## Extent of Reverse Transfers

Burton Clark (1960), in his study of a California junior college during the 1950s, was the first scholar to note the presence of undergraduate reverse transfers. Ten years later, Heinze and Daniels (1970) documented the presence of reverse transfers on a national level but did not differentiate between undergraduate and postbaccalaureate reverse transfers. In their 1969 survey of forty-six community colleges, they found that almost 10 percent of the students were reverse transfers. More than ten years later Hudak (1983) found that over 16 percent of students in 305 two-year colleges were reverse transfers (again, with no differentiation between URTSs and PRTSs). This aggregate figure disguised tremendous variability at the institutional level, where reported enrollment of reverse transfers ranged from less than 3 percent to as high as 65 percent. Also, the growing percentage of reverse transfers is indicated by the findings of de los Santos and Wright (1989). They found the percentage of reverse transfers enrolled in the Maricopa Community College District was 21.2 in the fall of 1982; by fall 1988 the percentage had increased to 45.5.

The most recent national data on undergraduate reverse transfers are from the National Center for Education Statistics (NCES). In its five-year study of students who began college in 1989–90 at a four-year school, NCES (1997) found that 13 percent transferred to "a less-than-four-year institution." Differing from students who transferred to another four-year school, URTSs didn't stay as long at the four-year school and were also more likely to stay out longer before enrolling at the second institution. Five years after starting college, 22 percent of the reverse transfers "had either completed a bachelor's degree . . . or were enrolled at a four-year school." Thus it appears that the percent of URTSs nationwide has ranged from over 9 percent to 16 percent since the late 1960s, with the most recent data indicating that they constitute about 13 percent of students at two-year colleges.

Data are also available that document the number of undergraduate reverse transfer students in some states. In fall 1981 almost 13 percent of Texas community college enrollments were students who had transferred from in-state universities (Texas College and University System, 1988). The Maryland Higher Education Commission found that between fall 1991 and fall 1992, over two thousand students transferred from four-year colleges in Maryland to community colleges in the state. In contrast, over seven thousand students transferred from community colleges to public four-year schools (Clagett, 1993). A study of fall 1992 Oklahoma students who transferred from both public and private institutions to public institutions within the state found that over 27 percent were URTSs (Oklahoma State Regents, 1993).

In addition to state and national studies, some district and single-institution studies also illustrate the presence of URTSs at particular schools. For example, Mitchell and Grafton (1985) looked at a representative sample of more than ten thousand students from the three colleges in the Los Rios Community College District and found that reverse transfer students constituted almost 20 percent of the students. Of these, 12 percent were URTSs; the rest were PRTSs.

The only statistic about the extent of PRTSs nationally is from the High School and Beyond/Sophomore cohort (1980–1993) database. Adelman (1998) found that 1.8 percent of students in this database had earned eighteen or more credit hours at a community college after first receiving a baccalaureate degree. However, the American Association of Community Colleges has estimated PRTSs to be between 10 to 20 percent of current community college students (Gose, 1997). PRTSs may be a growing phenomenon because of the increasing percentage of the general population with a baccalaureate degree. In 1990, approximately one out of five people had at least a baccalaureate degree ("Educational Attainment. . . ," 1998, p. 19). Another reason for the growth of PRTSs may be that many baccalaureate holders do not hold a job in the field of their degree. In 1990, almost 40 percent did not (Grubb, 1996, p. 97). It is possible that some PRTSs who switched job fields are pursuing in the two-year college the job-related training they did not get in their baccalaureate program.

Several states have documented the extent of PRTSs' enrollment in their state. For example, in 1984 PRTSs in Maryland community colleges ranged from less than 1 percent at small, rural colleges to over 23 percent in a suburban college located near the District of Columbia (McConochie, as cited in Lambert, 1994). According to the Illinois Community College Board, in 1996 approximately 33,000 of almost 350,000 Illinois community college students had a bachelor's degree or higher, up almost 2,000 from 1995 (Illinois Board of Higher Education, 1998; Illinois Community College System, 1997).

In single-institution studies looking only at PRTSs, the percentage of students has ranged from seven to almost twenty-five. For example, Ross (1982) found that in fall 1981, 13 percent of Piedmont Virginia Community College's credit students had a bachelor's degree or higher. Eight years later Klepper (1991) found the percentage had increased to over 24 percent. Quinley and Quinley (1997) studied a large, urban community college in North Carolina and found that during 1993–1996, over 7 percent of the students enrolled for credit each year had at least a bachelor's degree. Similarly, Townsend (1998) found that in fall 1996, over 7 percent of the students enrolled for credit at a technical institute in the Mid-South were PRTSs.

There is also limited evidence to indicate that reverse transfer is not an exclusively American phenomenon. Vaala (1991) noted the presence of undergraduate reverse transfers in her study of student attendance patterns at one two-year college in southern Alberta, Canada.

## Demographic Characteristics of Reverse Transfers

Generalizing about the demographic characteristics of reverse transfers is difficult because the data collected and their categorization are often inconsistent from study to study. Moreover, findings regarding race and ethnicity vary considerably because of a given community college's location.

Age is the one characteristic where some consistency emerges. For example, in her study of 465 URTSs who transferred to Tarrant County Junior College in Texas in fall 1984, Jackson (1990) found their ages to range from 18 to 65, averaging slightly under 26. Kajstura and Keim (1992), in their study of 296 reverse transfers at ten Illinois community colleges in 1989, found a similar age for URTSs—slightly over 27. As would be expected, all studies distinguishing between URTSs and PRTSs found a significantly higher age, about 10 years, for the latter group: 36 as opposed to 26 (Jackson, 1990) and 37 as opposed to 27 (Kajstura and Keim, 1992). The representational accuracy of these ages is indicated by the finding of Slark (1982) of an average age of 31.6 years for reverse transfers (both URTSs and PRTSs) for 237 students who were attending Santa Ana College (California) in 1982. However, a substantially lower figure is reported by Hogan (1986), who, working with a population of 2,673 students, found the average age to be 26.7; only 21 percent of these were PRTSs.

On the basis of gender, no definitive statement seems possible, with some studies reporting a majority of males (for example, Swedler, 1983; Brimm and

Achilles, 1977; Slark, 1982); and other studies finding more females (Hill-Brown, 1989; Hogan, 1986; and Kajstura and Keim, 1992).

PRTSs are also more apt to be married, have children, and be of a higher socioeconomic status than URTSs (Berg, 1984; Boyd, 1983; Jackson, 1990). They may also differ in the number of years to complete a two-year degree, with PRTSs completing the degree in less time (Delaney, 1995).

## Academic Performance at the Two-Year College

Studies have consistently demonstrated that URTSs as a group increased their grade point averages (GPAs) after transferring to the community college. Additionally, those in previous academic difficulty at the university improved their GPAs when they transferred back, particularly if to a different university. For example, a study by Brimm and Achilles (1977) focused on the "second chance" or "salvage" community college function for a group of 195 URTSs who had left the university (not identified) with an average GPA of 1.43. The students' academic performance significantly improved, with their average GPA increasing to 2.56, by more than one letter grade at the community college. For the ninety-one students who then returned to the university, there was a more moderate improvement, with the mean GPA for all hours subsequently attempted being 1.86, an increase of nearly half a letter grade.

Swedler (1983) found that among Northern Illinois University (NIU) transfer students in 1975–76, 15 percent (269) were reverse transfers prior to enrolling at NIU. The reverse transfers who had been in academic difficulty at their initial university before transferring to the community college (45 percent of the group) raised their GPA from 1.59 at the university to 2.99 at the community college. Those students who had not been in previous academic difficulty also showed improvement at the community college, with their average GPA increasing from 2.64 to 3.17. For those URTSs in previous academic difficulty who then went to NIU, 74 percent were successful, earning a GPA of 2.0 or higher. The overall mean GPA at NIU for all URTSs who had previously been unsuccessful at the university was 2.39. A factor affecting success for later university performance of URTSs was choosing a different university the second time around. In such cases Swedler found the likelihood of success to be twice that of returning to the same university. Gregg and Stroud (1977) made a similar finding for URTSs in North Carolina.

The academic performance of PRTSs has not been an issue, as these students have already demonstrated the ability to complete a baccalaureate degree.

## Students' Comparison of their Two-Year and Four-Year Experiences

A consistent finding in virtually all studies of reverse transfer students is their higher degree of satisfaction with certain aspects of the two-year experience than they had experienced in the university. For example, Kuznik (1972) found that the majority of URTSs in Iowa felt that the community college environment was less competitive, the curriculum more relevant to career plans, and attention more focused on the needs of individual students. Losak (1980), working with URTSs in Florida, found significantly higher satisfaction with the community college experience in eleven components, which can be grouped as clarity in instructional presentation and expected learning outcomes, a supportive environment that encouraged genuinely open student-faculty interaction and attention to individual concerns, and smaller class size. In a similar vein, Hill-Brown (1989) found that the "less competitive, more personalized atmosphere and relevant course offerings at community colleges" (p. 155) made them more desirable to reverse transfer students. Vaala (1991) found that undergraduate reverse transfer students in Alberta, Canada, particularly stressed their preference for the supportive faculty found in the two-year college.

Kajstura and Keim (1992), in their survey of both types of Illinois reverse transfers, found much the same patterns of preference for community colleges. Townsend's (1998) survey of degree-seeking PRTSs in a technical institute revealed that students were highly satisfied with both their four-year and two-year college experiences. However, they were far less satisfied with the four-year college's "counseling or job placement," "the financial cost of attending," and "development of my work skills" than at the two-year college. She also interviewed seven PRTSs, all of whom verbalized strong satisfaction with their two-year college experience, commending in particular the faculty as compared to four-year college faculty.

## Institutional Rationales for Admitting Reverse Transfer Students

Acceptance of reverse transfer students raises questions of institutional mission, particularly for the public two-year college. Under the rubric of serving the entire community, the college can easily accept these students. But for many people a basic mission of the community college is to serve those people who did not do well enough in high school to attend a four-year college or who left high school, went to work, and decided years later to attend college. Serving people who were academically qualified enough to have already been accepted to a four-year school, as in the case of URTSs, or who have previously completed an undergraduate degree, as with PRTSs, may conflict with the institution's primary mission.

Initially, undergraduate reverse transfers were admitted into the community college under the rubric of providing a second chance to students who had not performed well academically at four-year schools. Considered "academically deficient" (Meadows and Ingle, 1968, p. 48), these students could be served by the community college undertaking a "salvage" (Heinze and Daniels, 1970) or "retread" function (Lee, 1975). Not all two-year schools were willing to admit these students. Those that did sometimes placed them on academic probation (Heinze and Daniels, 1970). Meadows and Ingle (1968) described Kennesaw Junior College's (Georgia) enrollment in fall 1966 of fifty-three reverse transfers, who were admitted because their high school achievement and SAT scores would have qualified them for admission anyway (p. 50). Most of these students did as well as or better than native students. In much more recent times Kingsborough Community College in Brooklyn, New York, has developed a special program for four-year students in academic difficulty at their school. From 1985–1993, over two thousand students were served by the New Start Program, with almost half having transferred from Brooklyn College (Winchell and Schwartz, 1993).

As single-institution studies began to be conducted about reverse transfers, it became apparent that not all undergraduate reverse transfers attended the two-year college because of academic difficulties at the four-year level. For example, Rooth (1979) found that only 5 percent of URTSs at Northampton County Area Community College were "in academic difficulty prior to transfer" (p. 1). Similarly, Slark (1982), in her study of reverse transfers enrolled at California's Santa Ana College (SAC) in spring 1982, found that "[r]everse transfer students who are attending SAC for transfer education . . . are seldom students who encountered academic difficulty at the four-year college" (p. 8). Rather, reverse transfers chose the two-year school because it was less expensive than the four-year school or because they had moved since they began college (Slark, 1982). Other reasons for transferring to a community college from a university included the desire to attend a smaller college and be prepared for a job more quickly (Benedict, 1987), indecision about a major (Renkiewicz, Hirsch, Drummond, and Mitchell, 1982), and the community college's "convenient location and flexible schedule" (Hill-Brown, 1989).

Thus published rationales for admitting undergraduate reverse transfers began to shift away from providing a second chance academically to meeting institutional needs for enrollment. For example, Hogan (1986) advocates admitting reverse transfers (of both types) because of the decline in traditional-age college students. Additionally, some two-year schools consciously seek to enroll URTSs as temporary transfers during summer sessions. Moraine Valley Community College in Illinois has actively recruited these students through mass mailings. In summer 1986 URTSs' enrollment generated almost five thousand credit hours for the college (Reis, 1987). Finally, as Catanzaro notes in Chapter Three, reverse transfers of both types can also replace the students who leave the two-year college, either through withdrawal or graduation.

The rationale for admitting PRTSs was rarely addressed during the 1960s and 1970s. However, in 1976 Rue stated that these students' need for "life long learning," fulfilled by attending the community college, meant that "the mission of the community college must be broadly and generously interpreted" (p. 27). Similarly, Knoell (1976), in noting the presence of numerous postbaccalaureate students in her study of enrollment patterns in California's two-year schools, stated that "continuing education for part-time adult students has become the dominant function of community colleges, with no resultant neglect of the occupational, transfer, and general education functions for more traditional students" (p. 8). In the 1990s reasons for admitting PRTSs included providing a "second chance" for PRTSs in the job market (Lambert, 1994; Quinley and Quinley, 1997) and providing corporate and continuing education for careers, seen as an "expanded mission" for the community college (Schmidt, 1998, p. A29) and one well supported by business and industry. Although not related to institutional missions, the admission of PRTSs has also been supported because of the community college's need for enrollment and more tuition dollars (Harris, 1997).

## Conclusion

According to Peter Sacks (1996), community colleges are the "A-Mart" of higher education. Presumably Sacks is doing a word play on K-Mart, a chain of discount stores designed to appeal to blue-collar customers. Although Sacks was probably being pejorative in his comparison, customers can receive good value at these stores, depending on their standards and needs. For reverse transfers, the image of community colleges as K-Marts seems to fit. The education these institutions provide is a good value for the price. As experienced consumers of higher education, reverse transfers know that the education they receive at a two-year college is a bargain hunter's delight. Evidence of their satisfaction has been found in a variety of single-institution studies and is also provided by their enrollment over several decades.

Their enrollment also illustrates how the traditional transfer paradigm in which the two-year college serves as a pipeline to the four-year college no longer adequately captures many two-year students' institutional attendance patterns. Rather, the more natural yet complex ordering principle of the "swirl" reflects the movement of many students, including reverse transfers. Not only two-year college administrators and faculty but also state and federal policy makers need to remember this principle as they evaluate the community college's role in higher education and establish criteria for determining the institution's success in meeting student needs.

## References

Adelman, C. "National Replication of Selected Variables in the University of Memphis Transfer Study." Paper presented at the symposium, "Reframing 'Student Transfer' in Higher Education: Implications for Policy and Research." ASHE Annual Conference, Miami, Nov. 1998.

Benedict, J. B. "An Analysis of Reverse Transfer Students from Illinois State University." Unpublished doctoral dissertation, Illinois State University, 1987.

Berg, G.N.M. "The Reverse Transfer, Lateral Transfer, and First-Time Community College Student: A Comparative Study." Unpublished doctoral dissertation, University of Southern California, 1984.

Boyd, E. L. "Reverse Transfers: An Emerging Curriculum Student Group in the North Carolina Community College System." Unpublished doctoral dissertation. North Carolina State University at Raleigh, 1983.

Brimm, J., and Achilles, C. M. "The Reverse Transfer Student: A Growing Factor in Higher Education." *Research in Higher Education,* 1977, *4* (4), 355–360.

Clagett, C. A. "GCC Transfers to Maryland Public Four-Year Colleges" (Research Brief RB93-15). Largo, Md.: Office of Institutional Research and Analysis, Prince George's Community College, May 1993. (ED 356 010)

Clark, B. R. "The 'Cooling-Out' Function in Higher Education." *American Journal of Sociology,* 1960, *65* (6), 569–576.

Delaney, M. A. "Reverse Registrants in Community Colleges." Unpublished doctoral dissertation, University of Connecticut, 1995.

de los Santos, A. G., and Wright, I. "Community College and University Student Transfers." *Educational Record,* 1989, *79* (3/4), 82–84.

de los Santos, A. G., and Wright, I. "Maricopa's Swirling Students: Earning One-Third of Arizona State's Bachelor's Degrees." *Community, Technical, and Junior College Journal,* 1990, *60* (6), 32–34.

"Educational Attainment of the U.S. Population by Racial and Ethnic Group, 1990." *Chronicle of Higher Education Almanac,* Aug. 28, 1998, p. 19.

Gose, B. "A Community College in Virginia Attracts Ph.D.'s—as Students." *Chronicle of Higher Education,* July 11, 1997, pp. A33–34.

Gregg, W. L., and Stroud, P. M. "Do Community Colleges Help Salvage Late-Bloomers?" *Community College Review,* 1977, *4* (3), 37–41.

Grubb, N. *Working in the Middle: Strengthening Education and Training for the Mid-Skilled Labor Force.* San Francisco: Jossey-Bass, 1996.

Harris, P. A. "Reverse Transfers in the Kentucky Community College System." Unpublished doctoral dissertation, University of Louisville, 1997.

Heinze, M. C., and Daniels, J. L. *The Transfer of Students into Community Colleges.* Hattiesburg: University of Southern Mississippi, 1970. (ED 050 723)

Hill-Brown, H. A. "An Institutional Case Study of Reverse Transfer Students." *Dissertation Abstracts International,* 1989, *51* (4), 1132. (AAC90-24174)

Hogan. R. R. "An Update on Reverse Transfer to Two-Year Colleges." *Community/Junior College Quarterly,* 1986, *10,* 295–306.

Hudak, E. M. "The Reverse Transfer Student: An Emerging Influence on the Community/Junior College Campuses." Unpublished doctoral dissertation, George Washington University, 1983.

Illinois Board of Higher Education. *From Public Universities, Fall 1994, to Community Colleges.* Springfield: Illinois Board of Higher Education, 1998.

Illinois Community College System: Facts About Community Colleges. [http://www.iccb.state.il.us]. Nov. 25, 1997.

Jackson, C. J. "Reverse Transfer Students: Students Who Transfer from Area Universities to the Junior College." Unpublished doctoral dissertation. University of North Texas, 1990.

Kajstura, A., and Keim, M. C. "Reverse Transfer Students in Illinois Community Colleges." *Community College Review,* 1992, *20* (2), 39–44.

Klepper, D. F. "A Descriptive Analysis of Completer Transfer Students at a Virginia Community College." Unpublished doctoral dissertation, University of Virginia, 1991.

Knoell, D. "Through the Open Door: A Study of Patterns of Enrollment and Performance in California's Community Colleges" (Report No. 76-1). Sacramento: California Postsecondary Education Commission, 1976.

Kuznik, A. "Reverse Transfers: Students Who Transfer from Four-Year to Two-Year Colleges." *Journal of College Student Personnel,* 1972, *13* (5), 425–428.

Lambert, R. Y. "College-Wide: Post-Baccalaureate Reverse Transfer Students Attending Baltimore Community Colleges." Unpublished doctoral dissertation, University of Maryland, College Park, 1994.

Lee, R. "Reverse Transfer: The 'Retread' Function in Community Colleges." Paper presented at the annual meeting of the American Educational Research Association, Washington, D.C., 1975.

Losak, J. "Student Comparisons of Educational Experiences at the Two-Year College and the University: A Preliminary Study." *Community/Junior College Research Quarterly,* 1980, 4 (4), 361–377.

Meadows, M. E., and Ingle, R. R. "Reverse Articulation: A Unique Function of the Junior College." *College and University,* 1968, 44, 47–54.

Mitchell, G. N., and Grafton, C. L. "Comparative Study of Reverse Transfer, Lateral Transfer, and First-Time Community College Students." *Community/Junior College Quarterly of Research and Practice,* 1985, 9, 273–280.

National Center for Education Statistics. *Transfer Behavior Among Beginning Postsecondary Students: 1989–94.* [http://nces.ed.gov/pubs97/97266.html]. June 1997.

Oklahoma State Regents for Higher Education. "Student Transfer Matrix, Fall 1992." Oklahoma City: Oklahoma State Regents for Higher Education, Sept. 1993.

Quinley, J., and Quinley, M. "Coming Back for Employable Skills: The Growing Trend of Four Year Graduates Attending Community Colleges as Credit Students." Teachers College, N.Y.: Community College Research Center, 1997.

Reis, E. *Reverse Transfer Project, Summer 1986: Technical Report.* Palos Hills, Ill.: Office of Institutional Research, Moraine Valley Community College, Feb. 1987. (ED 289 537)

Renkiewicz, N. K., Hirsch, P. M., Drummond, M. E., and Mitchell, G. N. *The Reverse Transfer Student: An Emerging Population.* Sacramento: Northern California Community College Research Groups, Los Rios Community College, 1982. (ED 223 3081)

Rooth, S. R. *The Reverse Transfer Student at Northhampton County Area Community College.* Tempe: Arizona State University, 1979. (ED 178 122)

Ross, R. A. *The Reverse Transfer Phenomenon at Piedmont Virginia Community College, Fall Quarter, 1981* (Report No. 3-82). Charlottesville: Piedmont Virginia Community College, 1982. (ED 216 758)

Rue, R. "Will It Be Held Against Me? New Horizons for the Grad-Undergraduate." *Community and Junior College Journal,* 1976, 47 (3), 26–27.

Sacks, P. *Generation X.* Chicago: Open Court, 1996.

Schmidt, P. "States Turn to Community Colleges to Fuel Economic Growth." *Chronicle of Higher Education,* June 6, 1998, pp. A29–A30.

Slark, J. Y. *Reverse Transfer Student Study.* Santa Ana, Calif.: Santa Ana College, Sept. 1982. (ED 221 248)

Swedler, J. A. "Reverse Transfers Who Return to a University: An Analysis of Their Academic Progress." *Community/Junior College Research Quarterly,* 1983, 7 (2), 131–137.

Texas College and University System. *Analysis of Student Transfer and Persistence: Technical Report.* Austin, Tex.: Texas College and University System Coordinating Board, 1988. (ED 294 630)

Townsend, B. K. "Reverse Diploma Transfer Students in a Technical Institute," American Educational Research Association Annual Conference, San Diego, Apr. 1998.

Vaala, L. "Attending a Two-Year College After Attending a Four-Year University in Alberta, Canada." *Community College Review,* 1991, 18 (4), 13–20.

Winchell, A., and Schwartz, C. P. *New Start Program 1993: Eighth-Year Report.* Brooklyn, N.Y.: Kingsborough Community College, 1993. (ED 366 380)

BARBARA K. TOWNSEND *is professor of higher education at the University of Missouri– Columbia. While a professor at the University of Memphis, she worked in the Office of Academic Affairs on transfer and articulation issues. She is a former community college faculty member and administrator.*

JOHN T. DEVER *is dean of instruction and student services at Blue Ridge Community College, Weyers Cave, Virginia.*

*Using the analogy of paradoxes, this chapter relates California's rich history and experiences with reverse transfers.*

# Paradoxes: California's Experience with Reverse Transfer Students

*Linda Serra Hagedorn, Consuelo Rey Castro*

Throughout its 145 years of statehood, the so-called Golden State has earned its reputation as a maverick, a leader—a state vastly different from the other forty-nine. Indeed, California may well have earned its reputation by its many paradoxes. For instance, although every environmental and weather condition except the Arctic tundra can be found somewhere in the state, newcomers continually flock to California for its temperate climate. In economic terms, despite its standing as the seventh largest economy in the world, one that is equal to that of Argentina, Mexico, and Australia combined (Richardson, 1997), California also has a higher poverty rate (16.7 percent) than the national average (13.8 percent) (Evangelauf, 1997).

The paradoxes of California are also reflected in the state's education policies and outcomes. Pickens (1989) pointed to "defective institutional arrangements" and identified "gaps in state policy [that] have led to uneven educational results and unfortunate contradictions" (p. 46). Paradoxically, California has managed to successfully achieve higher college completion rates than the national averages while at the same time ranking 41st among the states in K–12 expenditures per pupil, having the largest class size in the nation, and experiencing low high school completion rates (Ed-Data, 1998; Evangelauf, 1997; Pickens, 1989).

This chapter will detail California's experiences and paradoxes that are related to reverse transfer by giving some general background and state history of postsecondary policies, as well as personal accounts. Because reverse transfer may be perceived as a paradox in itself, the state of California may provide the ideal case study. Throughout the chapter, we have broadly defined reverse transfer students as anyone enrolling in a community college with previous credits from a four-year institution (or equivalent). Table 2.1 provides a definition matrix of the various types of reverse transfer students.

## Historical Context

The presence of reverse transfers in California has been noted for several decades. For example, a 1979 report from the University of California (UC) indicated that more UC students transferred to the community colleges than community college students transferred to UC (Kissler, 1980). A 1985 study of the Los Rios Community College District of Northern California found that reverse transfer students constituted 20 percent of the student population (Mitchell and Grafton, 1985). Currently, the best estimate of reverse transfers in California includes about 116,000 students (8.0 percent of total enrollment) who hold at least a bachelor's degree and an additional 40,000 students (2.8 percent of total enrollment) who enrolled with college credits from another institution. However, officials from the chancellor's office caution that these figures are based solely on student applications and likely underestimate the number of California residents who fit under the broad "reverse transfer umbrella" definitions listed in Table 2.1. Because the enrollment status of over 127,000 students was classified as "uncollected/reported or not applicable," it seems likely that reverse transfers are underestimated (Chancellor's Office, 1996).

The California Master Plan. The unique history of California's postsecondary educational system began when Clark Kerr, the president of the Uni-

### Table 2.1. Definition Matrix of Reverse Transfer Students

| Student Nomenclature | Definition * |
| --- | --- |
| Undergraduate reverse transfer | Student with previous college credits from a four-year institution who enrolls in a community college for purposes of future transfer or vocational credits |
| Concurrently enrolled transfer | Student who enrolls in both a community college and a four-year college at the same time |
| Summer sessioner (temporary transfer) | Student regularly enrolled in a four-year college or university who enrolls in summer school at a community college with the intention of using (transferring) the credits toward a degree program at the four-year college |
| Foreign diploma | Student with a degree from a non-U.S. institution who enrolls in a community college |
| Postbaccalaureate reverse transfer | Student enrolling in a community college for (1) credit course work for purposes of career change, career advancement, career enrichment, or technology updates, despite holding a bachelor's, master's, or doctoral degree or (2) for recreational or avocational purposes |

versity of California, and a group of prominent educational leaders developed the famous Master Plan. California's Master Plan of 1960, incorporated in the Donohoe Act of 1961, established a "social contract" with the citizens of the state, which promised a low-cost college education to all eligible citizens (Richardson, 1997). The Master Plan effectively created a three-tiered system entitling the top 12.5 percent of California's high-school students admittance into the University of California System; the top 33 percent would be guaranteed admittance into the California State System, leaving the Community College system to provide universal access to all (Education Code, Section 2251; McCurdy, 1994). The Master Plan was a guarantee to all qualified California residents of a tuition-free and affordable undergraduate space (Pickens, 1995). The Master Plan was a successful public policy that created an enviable system of postsecondary governance while establishing a community college network of locally governed and financed institutions.

**Proposition 13.** California postsecondary policies changed with the passage of Proposition 13 in 1978. Juxtaposed beside the Master Plan, Proposition 13 created the perfect California paradox. The stated purpose of Proposition 13 was to grant property tax relief to California landowners. Unfortunately, the tax relief was accomplished at the expense of local government's ability to raise the necessary revenues for education, thus threatening the state's ability to fulfill its social contract to Californians. Under Proposition 13, local property taxes were directly funneled to the state, leaving the allocation of funds for community colleges state-controlled and enrollment-based. The purse strings of locally elected trustees thus came under the control of the state legislature. With property taxes reduced by 57 percent, the California Community College system experienced severe financial problems (McCurdy, 1994; Richardson, 1997). By 1984, it became apparent that community colleges could no longer afford to be totally free of tuition or enrollment fees. Thus in 1984 California community colleges levied the first general fee in their history—$5.00 per unit (Trombley, 1993).

**California Recession.** The next significant event was the passage of Assembly Bill 1725 in 1988. The Community College Reform Act was to supply $140 million to community colleges over the next two years and to clarify the true mission of the California Community College System (McCurdy, 1994). But AB 1725 was not sufficient to rescue the ailing community college system. Between 1990 and 1994, the state experienced a severe recession in which approximately 868,000 jobs and more than 43,000 businesses were lost (Richardson, 1997). In 1992–93 the community college system experienced a severe blow by receiving approximately $80 million less in funding than anticipated (McCurdy, 1994). The California recession was presenting yet another paradox: the community college system that was at one time the envy of the nation appeared to be close to collapse.

At the same time another paradox emerged in the state of California. During an economic downturn characterized by escalating unemployment and increases in the adult population, enrollment in the community colleges declined. Historically, such economic conditions triggered an increase in the number of enrolled students. According to the chancellor's office (More and Petrossian, 1996) the decline was due in part to the inability of the community college system to maintain the previous level of operations due to revenue shortfalls.

## The Differential Fee

With colleges facing impending doom, Governor Pete Wilson enacted legislation that would once again cast the state of California in a unique light. As of January 1993, student fees were raised from $6 to $10 per unit, and the $60 fee cap was removed. Prior to 1992, the fee cap limited fees to $60, regardless of the number of credits taken. After the California legislature passed the new fee structure, students were charged a uniform amount per credit. Additionally, students with a baccalaureate or higher degree were required to pay a $50 per unit "differential fee" (Lee, Jones, Brazil, and Puglisi, 1993; Trombley, 1993). Wilson and others behind the bold differential fee believed that degree holders were taking courses only for personal enrichment rather than job training or for serious academic reasons. The assumptions were that "baccalaureate holders in the community college system . . . were 'rich housewives' who wanted to study French so they could converse with waiters on their next European vacations" (Trombley, 1993, p. 2). State Assembly Speaker Willie Brown argued further that "it doesn't make sense to give valuable space to people who already have bachelor's degrees while we deprive first-time students of the opportunity to go to college" (Trombley, 1993, p. 2). Although local trustees, administrators, faculty, and student organizations stood firmly opposed, the differential fee received wide support by prominent state officials and governing bodies, including the California Postsecondary Education Commission (CPEC); David Mertes, Chancellor of the Community College System; Tom Hayden, chairman of the Assembly Higher Education Committee; and state senator Gary Hart (Trombley, 1993).

Almost immediately after the implementation of the differential fee, the community colleges experienced a severe decline in enrollment. According to the chancellor's office, about sixty thousand students with bachelor's degrees dropped out, ostensibly as a consequence of the additional fee (Trombley, 1993). At Napa Valley Community College total enrollment dropped 11 percent (Yue, 1997), while at Pierce College (located near Los Angeles) the drop was a dramatic 18 percent (McCurdy, 1994). Evening enrollments at Sacramento's Los Rios College dropped more than 14 percent, and the district lost almost half of its baccalaureate-holding students (Lee and others, 1993). At Foothill College, enrollments declined by 15 percent (Trombley, 1993). Although the increase in fees and the addition of the differential fee hit some colleges especially hard, all were affected. The chancellor's office estimated that enrollments declined by 8.8 percent (Mery, 1994). Indeed, the differential fees did accomplish the intended goal of limiting the enrollment of baccalaureate-

and-beyond degree holders. However, it took very little time before the reasoning that preceded the implementation of the fee was shown to be fallacious. The majority of reverse diploma students were *not* taking courses for frivolous reasons, but rather for job training or for upgrading of work-related skills. The Board of Governors reported that "prior to 1993, . . . two of every three community college students who already had baccalaureate degrees were enrolled to learn job skills" (More and Petrossian, 1996, p. 4). A monumental paradox emerged: the policy that was designed to pull the community colleges up from the depths of financial devastation was instead pushing them down deeper into the mire.

Even though the differential fee could be waived for "displaced" workers or homemakers or students on public assistance, very few students took advantage of the waivers or were even aware of their existence (Tronvig, 1993). The bottom line was that approximately 41 percent of the students with bachelor's degrees dropped out. However, according to interview sources at several California Community Colleges, because no effort was made to check for previous college degrees, an unknown number of reverse diploma students purposely "forgot" about their degrees when enrolling for classes, thus circumventing any additional fees.

## Personal Accounts

We soon discovered that due to a dearth of documentation and research, it was not possible to rely solely on the literature to understand reverse transfer in the state of California. To fill in the gaps of knowledge, we conducted interviews at three California community college campuses with students, former students, administrators, and decision makers. We sought individuals who had experienced reverse transfer, were familiar with California's history regarding the topic, or could inform us of their institution's present stance with respect to reverse transfer students. Our first interview site was located in a rural area north of San Francisco. The second college was located in a lower-socioeconomic area of Los Angeles, while the third college was located in a medium-sized town located approximately fifty miles northwest of Los Angeles.

We identified present and former students through a snowballing procedure. The first author of this chapter, a university professor teaching graduate education classes to community college instructors, requested her students to poll members of their community college classrooms to identify students fitting the criteria who would be willing to be interviewed. All willing participants were subsequently telephoned and their qualifications reevaluated. Further, we asked the students if they could recommend others who would fit our criteria. We subsequently interviewed those students whose experience appeared to add to our understanding. Eight interviews were conducted in person; an additional six students were interviewed on the phone.

Of all of our interviews, those of former reverse diploma students from the differential fee era told the most poignant stories. Their stories present rich pictures of a cruel paradox—academically able students who were seeking college classes but were discouraged through artificially constructed financial barriers.

## Postbaccalaureate Reverse Transfer Students

In Northern California we interviewed a woman we will call Nancy. When discussing the early 1990s, Nancy wanted us to know that the happy, secure individual we saw today was not the same person who existed during the differential fee era. In 1993, Nancy was a young mother with an aging bachelor's degree in biology from the University of California in Berkeley. Nancy explained that she had married shortly after college and had spent four years as a homemaker. When Nancy's marriage failed, her bachelor's degree did little to help her find appropriate employment that would support her and her two young children. In her words:

> What good is a B.A. in biology? I mean I couldn't be a doctor or a nurse or anything like that. So what good is it? I applied for a position with a bank, but I had no experience. I told them I had a BA in biology and they just said, "Yes, well we don't have much need for biologists here."

Nancy knew she needed training. Hearing about the dental hygiene program offered at a local community college, Nancy decided to apply. Then she heard about the differential fee. Again, Nancy's own words sum up her feelings: "I always thought the community colleges were next to free to California residents. The unfairness of the situation was unbelievable. What do you mean I have to pay $50 per credit more than everybody else?" In response to our query regarding the availability of waivers, Nancy looked at us incredulously and said, "I never knew about any waivers."

We interviewed another student in the Los Angeles area named Paul. Paul's story was slightly different. Paul had a degree from California State University at Northridge in political science. Although he was employed as a real estate agent, the California recession made it more and more difficult to earn enough commissions to support his family adequately. Paul said he "saw the writing on the wall" and began to investigate alternate careers.

> I thought maybe something in electronics. I went to the [local community] college to talk to someone about my options. Because my work kept me busy in the evenings I wanted morning classes. But they were few and full. The colleges were cutting back and I guess my situation didn't particularly interest anyone willing to help. I waited a few semesters and tried again, this time with a little more success.

The differential fee also troubled Paul. Although he said he was willing to pay the fee, he felt "abused and discriminated against." Paul understood and even agreed with the concept of a progressive fee structure but questioned if the differential fee was progressive or merely designed to penalize degree holders who were not financially secure. Paul would have been more supportive of a sliding fee structure based on personal income than one based on educational attainment alone.

All interviews with postbaccalaureate reverse transfer students regarding the differential fee era summed up the policy with the word *unfair.* Even students who were taking courses for personal enrichment or pleasure (graduate recreational or avocational students) felt the fee was unfair. One interview subject had the following comments on her personal enrichment courses:

> Why should the college care if I have a degree or not? If I want to take ballroom dancing, my degree is totally immaterial. If my dance partner who is also taking ballroom dancing doesn't have a degree, why should he pay less? Is he enjoying the class less? If they don't want people to take classes for enjoyment, then they just shouldn't offer classes like that.

The differential fee was abolished in spring 1996 and became a chapter in state history that most California policymakers would rather not remember. Soon after the differential fees were lifted, community college enrollments began to climb. According to administrators in the colleges we contacted, enrollment levels appear to be recovering to their "pre-differential fee" levels and are increasing quickly.

In the late 1990s students with a baccalaureate degree or higher appear to be attending the community colleges for slightly different reasons than their counterparts during California's recession days. According to our interviews with administrators and students, technology updates are a major goal. One of the administrators described his college as a "technology broker" in the eyes of many of the students:

> People are seeing their degrees age into obsolescence and they must get training to keep current. Reverse diploma students want to upgrade themselves. Their education has aged, and new developments are forcing them to look at new ways to get old jobs done. Their present jobs are requiring new technology, and they need background work to bring them up to par with newer workers. It's not fluff . . . it's survival.

## General Reverse Transfer Students

Up to this point, we have concentrated on postbaccalaureate reverse transfer students. But California's general reverse transfer students also have interesting stories. There are numerous reasons why students may transfer into a community college after experience at a four-year institution. Our interviews with present reverse transfer students and college administrators revealed several broad categories: financial, emotional, and academic.

**Financial Reasons for Transferring.** Students forced to leave college because of financial problems are not unique to California. However, the state's severe economic recession in the early 1990s is at least partially responsible for many of the financially motivated recent reverse transfers in the state. It must be noted, however, that California public college tuition costs for state residents remains the lowest in the nation. Nevertheless, community college fees are still lower than the other two public systems and considerably less than California's private institutions. For example, at the time of this writing, the University of California, Los Angeles charged undergraduates $3,863 in registration and educational fees, while the equivalent annual fee for students at the California State University was $1,584.

**Emotional Reasons for Transferring.** Most students leave their four-year college for reasons that can be termed *emotional*. This umbrella term includes areas such as homesickness or difficulty adjusting to college life, immaturity, and the irresponsible use of substances. Again, there is very little reason to believe that California students are different from students in other states. However, it may be that California's large proportion of minority students presents some unique circumstances. For example, in 1997 California passed Proposition 209, which ended all use of race or ethnicity in admissions, support programs, or related service. We interviewed an administrator in a large, urban community college in a largely Hispanic area and learned that, prior to the passage of California's Proposition 209, some of Los Angeles's most promising minority high school seniors were courted and offered scholarships at California's best universities. But some of these students left the four-year college, opting instead to enroll in the less prestigious community college. The administrator offered the following explanation:

> The students weren't necessarily having trouble in an academic sense but were basically uncomfortable. I guess they were just not ready for university life. They were used to their high schools, their neighborhoods, and their community where people looked and acted like them . . . in the university they were an oddity . . . they didn't fit in.

We spoke to several reverse transfer students, asking them why they had left their four-year institutions. Even when financial reasons were cited, there also seemed to be an emotional reason in tandem. Gina was typical:

> Why did I leave Cal State? Well there were many reasons actually. It was my first time away from home and I kind of went wild. My grades were OK the first semester, but the second semester things started to get worse and by third semester my grades were terrible. I was afraid I might not make it. There were financial reasons too. I needed to stop and think about what I was doing there before the loans got much bigger.

**Academic Reasons for Transferring.** Some students enrolled in the community college because they experienced problems keeping pace academically at their four-year institution. Transferring may appear more honorable than leaving in disgrace or admitting total defeat. We found that students citing the need for remedial course work or other academically related criteria usually had an emotional component intermixed. Wayne was a junior at the University of Southern California (USC) when he was interviewed. As a USC freshman, Wayne told us he had severe academic problems during his first semester that caused him to drop his courses without credits. He enrolled in a community college for two years and then returned to USC as a confident junior. In many ways, Wayne is atypical. He is from a middle-class background and attended a suburban community college that many would consider affluent. Wayne is also the son of two USC graduates who expected him to follow in their footsteps. Despite the particulars, Wayne's blend of remedial and emotional problems is familiar for reverse transfer students:

> I was going to USC but I wasn't keeping up. I guess I just never really learned to study. I got by easily in high school but it was different at USC. I thought I should leave before I was a total failure. Before that time I never thought about going to a community college. In my family, it was expected that all of us would go to USC. But either I wasn't ready or I didn't know how to do it. I grew up at [the community college]. The classes were small and I seemed to be able to keep up easily. I promised myself I would be a USC grad and I came back and now I am going to do it!

## Goals of Reverse Transfers

Among the general reverse transfers, we found a difference in goals by age. Young students who immediately enrolled in a community college after attending four-year institutions intended to transfer back to a four-year college. Older students who had let years intervene between their four-year experience and the community college seemed to favor vocational or two-year programs that did not require subsequent transfer. We found no apparent differences by gender or ethnicity.

**Summer Sessioners or Temporary Transfers.** Some four-year college students "transfer" to two-year colleges during the summer to supplement credits or course work at their regular four-year institution. Called *temporary transfers* in Chapter One, these students are labeled *summer sessioners* in this chapter. We looked for unique aspects that might set California's summer sessioners apart from their counterparts in other states. In spite of California's large proportion of Asian students, we found them overrepresented among summer sessioners. Despite Asians' overrepresentation, their reasons for enrolling during the summer were the same as those cited by other students—most wanted to earn their degree as economically and as quickly as possible. They used the community college as a convenient and inexpensive way to acquire additional necessary credits toward their bachelor's degree. Again and again throughout the interviews with summer sessioners, the word *cheap* was used. Another obvious trend was taking courses that filled general requirements but were not in the student's major discipline.

Many of the students were pleased with their community college courses. The relative ease and quality of the programs surprised some. Positive terms used by students included *smaller classes, enthusiastic professors, no differences, shorter lines,* and *quick* and *cheap.*

However, some students were disappointed with their community college experience. A young Hispanic female summer sessioner from the University of California described her motives and feelings as follows:

> The community college is not very challenging. The professors have low expectations as compared to UC. I think my high school was harder. One of the problems is that many of the students are just out of high school. The reading load is very light. I am taking this course to fill a remaining degree requirement. I just wish the course was more challenging.

We learned that all three of the campuses we studied prepared for the summer sessioners by scheduling extra sessions of the courses most demanded by these students. Typical courses were basic requirements in English and mathematics, history, economics, foreign languages, and chemistry. Furthermore, the summer schedules of the community colleges are compiled with the schedules of the local four-year schools in mind. One of the administrators described the summer sessioners as follows:

> They come on campus and really take advantage of us. These kids are smart, and they know the system. They are usually the first in line to see the counselor and more aggressive when they need help. It is not uncommon for these students to come multiple summers until they have exhausted the courses that will transfer directly. I think they see us as a great bargain.

**Foreign Diplomas.** Although students with foreign diplomas may technically be postbaccalaureate reverse transfer students, their plights and reasons for enrollment in a community college more closely resemble the general reverse transfer students. The holders of these degrees frequently seek educational opportunities and American credentials because many foreign degrees are not recognized in the United States. In addition, even if the foreign degree is recognized, many recent immigrants require ESL (English as a second language) classes in order to acquire or maintain a job in the United States. Because California has a very high proportion of immigrants and speakers of other languages, foreign diploma students are common on the state's community college campuses. Interviews with administrators and faculty revealed some programs that tend to have much higher proportions of foreign diploma students. For example, at one college the electron microscopy and biology program attracted a large proportion of students with medical degrees from foreign institutions. In many cases the foreign credentials were not honored in the United States; in other cases the students sought practical experience and a degree program that would lead to employment.

## Conclusion

California community colleges are frequently criticized for failing to success-fully prepare and transfer a greater number of students to four-year institu-tions. Interestingly, this criticism may befit all institutions of higher education because the "de facto transfer rate from lower to upper division [at four year institutions] is no better than that of public two year and private junior col-leges" (Adelman, 1988, p. 41). Perhaps this is one of the possible explanations for national and state trends indicating that the number of reverse transfers in California's 106 community colleges will skyrocket. Yet another paradox is emerging. Similar to other states, the California community colleges were designed to serve as a gateway to postsecondary education. However, in grow-ing numbers the community colleges are serving as an intermediate or even terminal educational outpost to growing numbers of education seekers. We can no longer assume a one-way, linear, and vertical progression of transfer (Piland, 1995). Paradoxically, the more the regional level of educational attain-ment rises, the more local residents seek education. In other words, an edu-cated society appreciates the value and utility of education and thus its members are more likely to continue to seek additional education throughout life. Education begets more education. Other social trends point to this con-clusion as well. Increases in the average life expectancy, years of gainful employment, and the number of lifetime careers all point to a growing need for lifelong learning. And, of course, there is the growing role of the technol-ogy explosion that forces people to retool, rethink, and reeducate. Additional trends such as increased societal mobility and changing familial patterns all point to the likely conclusion that community colleges will be sought to assist in the personal, professional, and emotional transformations of California cit-izens regardless of their previous educational experiences.

## References

Adelman, C. "Transfer Rates and the Going Mythologies." *Change,* Jan./Feb. 1988, pp. 39–41.
Chancellor's Office, California Community Colleges. "The Effectiveness of California Community Colleges on Selected Performance Measures." Sacramento: Accountability Unit, Policy Analysis and Development Division, Oct. 1996.
Ed-Data, Education Data Partnership. "California's Rankings, 1995–96, 4/97." [http://www.ed-data.k12.ca.us//calrankings.html]. June 1998.
Evangelauf, J. (ed.). Almanac Issue [Special issue]. *Chronicle of Higher Education,* 1997, 59 (1).
Kissler, G. R. "Trends Affecting Undergraduate Education in the University of California." Paper presented at the Board of Regents of the University of California Committee on Educational Policy, Oct. 1980.
Lee, B. S., Jones, J. C., Brazil, B., and Puglisi, V. *Limiting Access by Degrees: Student Profiles Pre and Post the Fees.* Sacramento, Calif: Los Rios Community College District, Office of Planning and Research, 1993. (ED 356 836)
McCurdy, J. "Broken Promises: The Impact of Budget Cuts and Fee Increases on the California Community Colleges." San Jose: California Higher Education Policy Center, Nov. 1994.

Mery, P. M. *City College of San Francisco Impact of BA-Degree Holder Fee on Credit Enrollments.* San Francisco: Office of Institutional Development, Research and Planning, 1994. (ED 380 162)

Mitchell, G., and Grafton, C. "Comparative Study of Reverse Transfer." *Community and Junior College Quarterly,* 1985, *9* (3), 273–280.

More, V. D., and Petrossian, A. S. *The New Basic Agenda: Policy Directions for Student Success.* Sacramento: California Community Colleges, Office of the Chancellor, 1996. (ED 401 957)

Pickens, W. H. "California Perspectives: Three Viewpoints." *Change,* Oct. 1989, pp. 43–51.

Pickens, W. H. *Financing the Plan: California's Master Plan for Higher Education 1960 to 1994—A Report from the California Higher Education Policy Center.* San Jose: California Higher Education Policy Center, May 1995.

Piland, W. E. "Community College Transfer Students Who Earn Bachelor's Degrees." *Community College Review,* 1995, *23,* 35–44.

Richardson, R. C. Jr. "State Structures for the Governance of Higher Education: California Case Study Summary." Technical report prepared for State Structures for the Governance of Higher Education and the California Higher Education Policy Center. [http://professionals.com/~chepc/california/calif2.html]. Spring 1997.

Trombley, W. H. *Public Policy by Anecdote: The Case of Community College Fees.* San Jose: California Higher Education Policy Center, 1993. (ED 356 806)

Tronvig, J. A. *The Impact of the Differential Enrollment Fee on Chaffey College Baccalaureate Students.* Rancho Cucamonga, Calif.: Chaffey Community College, 1993. (ED 361 021)

Yue, P. Y. "Napa Valley College Enrollment Trends Credit Students Fall 1990 to Fall 1997 and Fall 1997, Detailed Demographics." Napa Valley, Calif.: Planning and Resource Development, Oct. 1997.

LINDA SERRA HAGEDORN *is assistant professor in the Center for Higher Education Policy Analysis in the School of Education at the University of Southern California, Los Angeles, and program chair of the concentration in community college leadership.*

CONSUELO REY CASTRO *is chair of the Social Science Department at East Los Angeles City College and a Ph.D. candidate at the University of Southern California, Los Angeles.*

*A president categorizes and profiles reverse transfer students at his institution and suggests ways to recruit them.*

# Understanding and Recruiting the Reverse Transfer Student: A Presidential Perspective

*James L. Catanzaro*

When Horatio Alger declared, "Go West, young man," over a century ago, he was, surely unwittingly, calling for more than the Westward Movement. He was encouraging what was already well under way: people moving about the country in every direction—to cities, to the Midwest, to the mountains, and finally to the real West. This now endemic movement has created suburban America, and it has led to the social dislocations of the twentieth century. In fact, modern Americans have become one of the most mobile people on earth, frequently changing their place of residence, work site, and even their college.

The average contemporary citizen changes venues and roles several times in a lifetime. So studies show that, at the beginning of a new age, nearly half of all students enrolled in postsecondary institutions in the United States will move to at least one other institution; one-third will enroll in three or more schools (McCormick and Carroll, 1997).

Some of this movement is directly accounted for by social mobility. Much of it is linear movement to four-year institutions from community and junior colleges as part of their established mission. This linear transfer population has been carefully tracked and studied. There is a paucity of information, however, on the students who enroll in a fall or spring term in a two-year institution after first studying at a four-year college or university. These reverse transfer students make up an important and diverse segment of most community college student populations.

As president of Chattanooga State Technical Community College (CSTCC) in Tennessee, I have become increasingly aware of these students' presence at the college. Based on focus groups and one-on-one conversations with some reverse transfers, I became aware of some variables affecting the percentage of reverse transfers at a two-year college. I also concluded that this classification of students breaks down into at least five primary subgroups. After presenting the variables, I will categorize these students, present a profile of a student from each category, and discuss effective ways to recruit reverse transfers.

## Variables Affecting Enrollment

As indicated in Chapter One, the current percentage of reverse transfer students, taken together, is unknown at the national level. Within individual community colleges or districts, however, it may be at least one-quarter of the students. For example, Baratta (1992) reported that between 1982–83 and 1989–90, reverse transfers constituted almost 25 percent of the students in the Contra Costa Community College District in California. The variables that apparently influence the size of this group are as follows:

Community college proximity to four-year schools
Comparative costs as related to student financial ability (the lower the family income, the more appealing the two-year college)
Consumer (dis)satisfaction with the area university; marketing by two-year colleges directed to this population
The offering of programs and courses that match one or more of the subgroup interests
Perceptions of the effectiveness of the placement services of the two-year college and publicized employment rates of graduates
Student academic success or lack thereof at the four-year school
Problems of social adjustment at the university, usually related to perceived negative experiences with certain faculty and even departments

## Categories of Reverse Transfer Students

I found the following types of reverse transfer students enrolled at CSTCC:

*Special purpose undergraduate reverse transfers:* four-year college students who enroll at the two-year college to fulfill special needs
*Technical degree undergraduate reverse transfers:* university undergraduate students who have reverse-transferred to earn a technical degree or certificate
*Enrichment postbaccalaureate reverse transfer students:* students with a four-year college degree who enroll in the community college for enrichment or for a specific personal objective, often quite some time after they have left the university
*Specific skills postbaccalaureate reverse transfer students:* students who have four-year college or university degrees but at a certain point need specific job-related skills offered by a two-year college

*Transient students:* students whose intermittent attendance in several settings suggests that they made choices based on comparative cost, proximity, and accessibility rather than a clear academic or career path

I selected one student from each subgroup enrolled at CSTCC in the 1997–98 academic year to query about reasons for his or her decision to reverse transfer. These students appeared to be representative of the subgroups. Clearly, these conversations did not yield information on which a college could determine policy, but they did provide useful insights into the thinking of some who choose to reverse the established pattern of college enrollment.

## Special Purpose Undergraduate Reverse Transfer Students

Donna, a sophomore in a local university, is still undecided about career and major. She reports maintaining a 3.2 GPA but she has not met the university's math and natural science requirements. So she is co-enrolled at CSTCC, hoping to find a more supportive environment in which to fulfill her math and science requirements with a greater likelihood of passing, indeed, with a greater likelihood of not pulling down her university GPA. Her experience in the two-year college, she asserts, has been so positive that she may fully transfer in and complete a career program, preferably in an allied health field.

She reports that other acquaintances who are reverse transfers from the same university say they will continue at the university after the community college meets their special needs. These needs appear to be principally in computer science (or literacy), remedial studies, and math and natural science. These students have enrolled at the two-year school (or co-enrolled) for one or more of the following reasons: the courses they sought at the four-year college were not offered at convenient times; they can reduce overall tuition costs if they take some of their work in a two-year college; they believe the community college courses are easier or, in any case, their grades won't be reflected on their university transcript and affect their GPA; they wish to avoid certain faculty at the university; or they are following friends or "inside information" that this is the way to go. They are likely to take one or two courses in a term and then not return to the community college, their goal having been met. A few like Donna leave the university and enroll solely in the community college, based on their experience or newfound academic and career goals.

## Technical Degree Undergraduate Reverse Transfer Students

Mandy has completed three years of a four-year degree in biology, having studied for more than five years at two universities. Recently she married and moved to Tennessee; she believes she now must have a job that pays more than $25,000 annually so she and her husband can have the lifestyle they desire.

Her answer: enroll at Chattanooga State in an allied health field, tough it out for two years, and earn the money and have the security she and her husband seek. Mandy appears to be the typical reverse transfer with a technical degree or certificate in mind.

These reverse transfers seek technical degrees or certificates in fields like nursing, graphic arts, engineering technology, and the like because they can be earned in two or fewer years; the students perceive the jobs in those fields as paying well, being available in any community, and offering job security. Technical degree students often come to the two-year college with a bachelor's degree; a few have earned an advanced degree. Commonly their university major is in a field in which placement is perceived to be difficult, compensation is reported to be low, or they have discovered that a graduate degree is essential to meet their career expectations. These students desire the more certain placement and often the higher wages and job security afforded through certification or the possession of specific technical skills gained through the community college.

## Enrichment Postbaccalaureate Reverse Transfer Students

Personal development is what Marge seeks from community college classes in the humanities. A mature woman with a successful husband and a degree in history, she likes the excitement of being in college again, especially with a number of peers who savor the collegiate experience they may have given short shrift to years ago. She will re-enroll each term as long as there is another exciting course to experience, a talked-about professor's course to take, and peers who plan to keep the experience going.

These reverse transfers who enroll in a community college for enrichment may indeed be long-term students, especially if their interest is a field like art where they can take (unless there are restrictions) the same courses over and over again in order to improve their skills. They often come first for the continuing education program the college offers, but in time they migrate to credit courses because they want depth of knowledge and intellectual challenge. Some simply glossed over the humanities on the way to a degree that set them on their career path. For them, courses in art, music, literature, philosophy, history, foreign languages, and so forth represent the opportunity for personal growth and acculturation. Many of these students are retired or are nonworking mothers. A few need a certain skill for a very specific and personal purpose: they plan to travel, for example, to France and they want an introduction to the language, history, and culture of the French, or a business leader or physician wants a pilot's license and enrolls in a community college for flying lessons and to prepare for the Federal Aviation

Administration exam. In general, these reverse transfers are mature, well-educated, dedicated students who set the standard for performance in their classes.

## Specific Skills Postbaccalaureate Reverse Transfer Students

An established engineer in a local division of a chemical company, Daryl has an engineering degree but earned it more than fifteen years ago. He wants to bring his formal engineering education current, and he wants exposure to cognate fields he has not explored: robotics and computer-integrated manufacturing. So he enrolled at Chattanooga State first to take a course or two. Now he wishes to complete the electrical-electronics engineering technology associate degree requirements so he can be brought up to speed comprehensively and become knowledgeable about the latest equipment in his field.

This subgroup of reverse transfers usually needs specific skills to advance in the workplace or needs to be refreshed in their discipline. They typically seek out courses in information science, engineering technology, management and the like, looking to update their knowledge and skills. Many have been (or soon will be) promoted to a supervisory position; many have encountered an obstacle to career development that they or their employers believe can be overcome by short-term, focused exposure to a specific discipline. Like Daryl, they are prepared to make the modest time investment (usually two evenings a week) necessary to add valued knowledge sets, including state-of-the-art workplace applications.

## Transient Students

Perhaps the largest group of reverse transfers consists of transient students. Their mobility may be related to their spouse's occupation or simply to the perception that the value of higher education is not in the traditional curriculum or degree; it is in forays here and there into the intellectual forest to harvest what is interesting and useful to them. They are more likely than not "twentysomethings." Their common response to the request that they put together an academic plan is, "That was then, this is now." Plans were needed by older generations of Americans; they don't fit New Age Americans.

Darrin is clearly a transient student. He has accumulated credits from two state universities, another community college, and now Chattanooga State. In his early twenties he earned some of the credits while in the military and the others as he has moved about the country to keep alive his hobby of hang gliding. As long as he can "do his thing," earn enough to have a place to stay and an off-road vehicle to take him where he wants to go, he is satisfied. College means learning about new things and it gives him the assurance, most likely mistakenly, that he is going somewhere in life. When gliding is over or marriage overtakes him, he thinks he will have a start on a more conventional life.

## Recruiting Reverse Transfer Students

The futurist, Willard Daggett, announced to the League for Innovation Workforce 2000 Conference in Anaheim, California, in 1997 that "community colleges will be the graduate schools of the 21st century." If so, many more reverse transfers will occur, and the two-year colleges of America will have to prepare for them. Clearly, changes in recruitment and marketing will be necessary to take advantage of this increasing interest in special courses, technical programs, and applied education.

Chattanooga State has already initiated these efforts. Because our fall term begins after the area university's term, we advertise in the university's student newspaper as well as the area media to attract special purpose students. This strategy is complemented by direct mail to selected target populations and billboards that emphasize the differential in cost and accessibility to the most sought-after courses.

Attracting university students to technical degree programs may be more challenging if the students are enrolled in four-year liberal arts programs. Many direct mail pieces sent from Chattanooga State to residents feature the benefits of certain career programs in ways that may well be attractive to degree holders or to those well on their way to the baccalaureate. These direct mail pieces are reinforced by television infomercials and specials that present, in compelling fashion, the career opportunities, benefits, and compensation for graduates in health occupations, computer technology, and a number of other high-paying, in-demand fields that require the community college experience.

Recruiting students with a baccalaureate degree for enrichment purposes requires new course development, as well as specific marketing. It may also require convenient, nontraditional sites. Certainly course titles and descriptions need to be modified, at the least. An excellent way to begin to recruit this subgroup is to form focus groups to find subjects of interest and determine if the standard course architecture has appeal. Perhaps a one-unit (two hours every other week) format, for example, is a more attractive format for computer literacy than the standard three-unit, three hours per week for a term—the structure common in American higher education. Most likely, an Internet or video delivery system will have greater appeal. Using a descriptive title in direct mail pieces such as "Making your Computer a Friendly Companion" may be more attractive than the plainer "Computer Literacy." Perhaps offering several of these courses targeted for returning students at a neighborhood church may work better than campus-based scheduling. Degree holders are already education-friendly; now the task is to find their specific enrichment interests and put the college's response (the course or program) within their reach.

Perhaps the easiest subgroup to speak to is the degree holder who needs further technical skills. At Chattanooga State we have engaged them through customized curricula designed with corporate partners. We have also created "institutes" to attract these students from the general population. Those with the greatest enrollment are in applied management, sustainability, and community leadership. These are vehicles for recruiting area residents who are in the middle of their careers and seek specific technical skills. The institutes attract degree holders because they offer real-life skills that students can use immediately as managers, professionals, elected officials, and so on. This subgroup seeks know-how and new knowledge sets principally in an executive training center setting and in time-compressed formats. They want the graduate experience without the traditional obstacles to learning that graduate programs present: program admission screens, the focus on theory, the two-year curriculum, the thesis or master's projects, and so forth. They see the community college that responds to them as their "graduate school" of choice.

Marketing to the final subgroup—transient students—is undoubtedly the greatest challenge. Knowing more about the values, attitudes, and behaviors of young adults in particular will help engage these students and direct them to an academic path. Usually these students appear without warning or preparation. Retaining them past a single semester should be a specific responsibility of college support staff. To achieve this, the college has to have mechanisms for identifying these students early on so counselor-adviser-faculty intervention can be attempted. Just as hang gliding may excite some students to make difficult lifestyle choices, so a certain program of studies may excite them to settle in and work to achieve a well-defined goal. A valuable assist can often come from student activities, intramurals, service learning, and other co-curricular experiences. These may provide the mechanism for converting the transient student to the persisting student motivated by a compelling purpose.

## Conclusion

The community college has for decades articulated a commitment to life-long learning. Educating reverse transfers should be, therefore, an important and natural part of this commitment. As we increasingly identify and follow these students, our understanding of how to support their ongoing learning needs will be enhanced. Perhaps in time we will have designated staff for the reverse transfers of our colleges. And the programs we offer will include an array of special learning packages like the Applied Management Institute of Chattanooga State. The institute consists of a one-year, fifteen-unit program designed for the new manager who has technical and workplace skills but little systematic, formal education on what effective management is on the shop floor, in the office bay, or the executive suite. The institute has one regular college instructor who coordinates the program. Most sessions are taught, however, by local corporate types who give the institute authentic applied management elements and external credibility. The institute is the college's answer to M.B.A. programs that a require at least two full years and a substantial theoretical understanding of business. It is well known that the typical M.B.A. graduate leaves with very limited workplace skills, and the degree is recognized by only a few employers as of value to them (except, of course, for upper-tier university M.B.A.'s). Programs of this sort are surely what Daggett had in mind for community colleges.

It is likely that further examination of the reverse transfer population will lead to other specific programmatic developments tailored for each subgroup. The reverse transfer represents a significant recruitment potential for two-year colleges. At Chattanooga State, as many students transfer in as out each year. This balance is found in a number of community colleges and statewide in California. In fact, in the early nineties, substantially more students transferred from the University of California and the California State University System to California community colleges than from the two-year institutions (California Postsecondary Education Commission, 1996). This may well be the common experience of community colleges in the twenty-first century.

## References

Baratta, F. *Profiles of District Transfers to University of California, California State University and St. Mary's College.* Martinez, Calif.: Contra Costa Community College District, Aug. 1992. (ED 349 066)

California Postsecondary Education Commission. "Progress Report on the Community College Transfer Function" (Report 96-4). Sacramento: California Postsecondary Education Commission, 1996.

McCormick, A. C., and Carroll, D.C. *NCES 97–266, Transfer Behavior Among Beginning Postsecondary Students: 1989–94.* Berkeley: MPR Associates, 1997. (ED 408 929)

*JAMES L. CATANZARO is president of Chattanooga State Technical Community College in Tennessee. He previously served as president of Triton College in Illinois, Lakeland College in Ohio, and Chaffey College in California.*

*This chapter analyzes the life circumstances and goals of postbaccalaureate reverse transfer students in an urban North Carolina community college.*

# The Urban Postbaccalaureate Reverse Transfer Student: Giving New Meaning to the Term *Second Chance*

*John W. Quinley, Melissa P. Quinley*

The community college has often been described as a second-chance institution for students who had failed in previous educational endeavors, who had stopped short of reaching a desired level of educational attainment, or who were required to improve their GPA before returning to a four-year institution.

However, another second-chance type of community college student, one whose characteristics are quite different from those just described, is one who enters the community college after having successfully completed a four-year degree or higher. These postbaccalaureate reverse transfer students (PRTSs) have already demonstrated their academic ability; many have distinguished themselves in their careers. They are looking for a second chance of a different sort. Some want to start a new career or a career on the side; others seek to begin their first economically successful job; a few want to explore what they really want to do for a career. Still others want to develop creative, self-enrichment interests, which are often related to career interests as well.

The research literature addresses this population to a limited extent, as Chapter One illustrates, but much more about this growing population needs to be understood. Prospective four-year college students and their parents, governmental policy developers and trustees, administrators and faculty in higher education—all join the research community in needing to know more about

The study reported in this chapter was conducted with financial support and editorial advice from the Community College Research Center, Institute on Education and the Economy, Teachers College of Columbia University.

this population. To increase understanding, this chapter reports selected findings from a study of PRTSs. The study employed two methodological approaches: (1) an examination of student records and (2) thirty-eight telephone interviews. Conducted in spring 1997, the interviews were with PRTSs attending a large urban community college in North Carolina. Only students who had completed fifteen or more hours at the college were included. The findings presented in this chapter focus on two major sections of the complete study: (1) the life circumstances and goals of the students and (2) profiles of the students.

## Life Circumstances and Goals

The study asked two general questions about the life circumstances of the thirty-eight four-year graduates attending the community college: (1) What was your background in terms of education and career before attending the community college? (2) What are (or were) your career and educational goals at the community college? Table 4.1 summarizes the responses, which are then explained in detail. To develop the table, we made judgments as to the assignment of primary categories across questions for each respondent.

### Table 4.1. Respondents' Backgrounds and Primary Community College Goals

| Item | Number | Percent |
|---|---|---|
| Major at four-year school | | |
| Liberal arts | 17 | 44 |
| Career | 21 | 56 |
| Career background after four-year graduation | | |
| Limited experience (less than two years) | 9 | 23 |
| Moderate experience (two to five years) | 10 | 27 |
| Extensive experience (more than five years) | 19 | 50 |
| Primary career goal at community college | | |
| Career exploration | 1 | 3 |
| Update skills for current job | 4 | 10 |
| Supplemental income | 3 | 8 |
| New career | 21 | 56 |
| Personal interest | 9 | 23 |
| Community college degree | | |
| Health-related | 7 | 18 |
| Technology area | 17 | 49 |
| Other | 12 | 33 |
| Degree intent | | |
| Yes | 18 | 47 |
| No | 17 | 46 |
| Undecided | 3 | 8 |

Note: Responses reported here reflect students' primary college goals only. The authors made judgments as to the assignment of primary categories across questions for each respondent.

**Major at Four-Year School.** More respondents had completed four-year degrees in career majors than in the liberal arts; 56 percent had graduated in career areas in their four-year schools. Eleven majors were represented, with business (six students) and education (three students) being the only areas with more than one student in a major. Forty-four percent of the students had earned a four-year, liberal arts degree. Psychology was the most common degree at five, followed by English, art-theater, and biology. Three respondents had earned a degree beyond the baccalaureate.

**Career Background.** The majority of respondents had considerable work experience before coming to the community college. Half of those responding to this item reported having worked in their field for more than five years. Within this group, the average number of years worked was sixteen; 27 percent reported working from two to five years, and 23 percent reported working less than two years.

**Primary Goal at Community College.** An analysis of the respondents' descriptions of their reasons for attending the community college led to five categories of educational goals: career exploration, current job skills update, supplemental income, new career, and personal interest. Almost eight in ten respondents reentered higher education at the community college level for goals related to employment. The majority of students sought to prepare for a new career; 10 percent sought to update skills for their current job, many of these for computer skills; 8 percent sought skills needed to earn supplemental income, mostly real estate majors; 3 percent matriculated to explore career areas; 23 percent entered the community college for personal interest or self-enrichment. Of these, personal interest courses in the arts were the most common.

Eleven out of thirty-eight respondents reported more than one primary area of educational goal. Students often saw multiple goals as linked, not discrete, categories. For example, some respondents who began their studies at the community college in order to secure a new career also reported that they intended to continue enrolling to keep their skills up to date. Other respondents entered the community college for personal interest, but this interest then led to the potential for supplemental income or a new career.

**Community College Major or Area of Interest.** The respondents' curriculum major or area of interest at the community college divided into three types: health-related, technical, and "other." The technical area saw the largest concentration of interest, with almost half of the respondents in this category. Within the technical area, the computer science, engineering, and paralegal majors held the most interest. In degree of interest, the health-related areas ranked second, with 18 percent of the respondents indicating an interest. Nursing was the only single academic program indicated by more than one respondent. The "other" category represented one-third of the total responses. This group included students taking personal interest classes (primarily art and literature-related) and students taking real estate classes.

**Degree Intent.** Forty-seven percent of the respondents initially intended to earn a community college degree, and 8 percent were undecided about their intent. Most respondents interested in a degree were enrolled in majors for which the related occupation required a license, including fire science, engineering, paralegal careers, law enforcement, physical therapy, dental hygiene, nursing, and real estate. Forty-six percent were not interested in a degree. Of these respondents, about one-third attended for career reasons.

**Relationship of Four-Year Degree to Community College Degree.** Table 4.2 summarizes the relationship between the four-year degree major and the community college major or area of interest. The majority of respondents who earned a four-year degree in the liberal arts (54.5 percent) or in the career areas (50 percent) enrolled in technical programs at the community college.

The category "other" had the second-largest number of respondents for both four-year liberal arts (36.4 percent) and career (37.5 percent) degree areas. The "other" category, included personal interest areas (primarily art and literature) and real estate. The health area at the community college saw 9.1 percent and 12.5 percent enrollment coming from the liberal arts and career four-year degree areas, respectively.

## Profiles of Students

We used open-ended interviews to get a description of the life circumstances that four-year graduates were facing prior to their decision to continue their education at the community college. The five educational goals identified in this study provided a framework to describe typical profiles of respondents. For several goal areas, the typical response pattern can be divided into subareas.

**Career Explorer.** To explore possible careers was the initial goal in entering the community college for two students, although only one reported it as the primary goal. One respondent felt certain that he was headed toward a career in some business-related area; the other student was uncertain, open to different career paths.

One of these respondents had earned a B.A. in journalism and worked for ten years in a newspaper marketing department selling ads, primarily in the construction trades area. After taking courses in several areas, he concluded that this prior experience might prove to be a good foundation for a career in real estate, either a new primary career or a source of supplemental income as a second job. He started by taking a few courses in real estate and insurance before engaging seriously in this major. In commenting about the choice to

**Table 4.2. Relationship of Four-Year Degree
and Community College Major or Interest**

| Four-Year Degree Area | Community College Major or Area of Interest | | |
| --- | --- | --- | --- |
| | Technical | Health | Other |
| Liberal arts (N = 11) | 6 (54.5 percent) | 1 (9.1 percent) | 4 (36.4 percent) |
| Career (N = 16) | 8 (50 percent) | 2 (12.5 percent) | 6 (37.5 percent) |

attend the community college, the respondent said, "It was a good place to try courses out to see how I might like them. The college made it economically feasible to try different things."

The other student in this category set aside a four-year degree in history to start a family. With no work experience and a degree in history, she soon realized that her career prospects were limited. Because she was undecided as to a possible career direction, she elected to take a wide variety of courses of personal interest to see if any area became a dominant interest. For this respondent, this strategy eventually led to enrollment in a paralegal program.

**Career Update.** Four respondents reported that they had reentered education at the community college level to update their skills for their current jobs. Two of these respondents explained that they enrolled in computer courses because competency in the latest computer applications had become a requisite for continuing success in their fields. The respondents, one an experienced real estate agent and the other a business education teacher, noted that their prior formal education did not include an adequate foundation in technology. They further noted that if their prior training had included more technological applications, that training would certainly be outdated today.

Three other respondents wanted to expand their knowledge in areas related to their current, primary jobs. A director of nursing enrolled in several work-related courses, including a class in workmen's compensation law. Another respondent, a teacher with a sociology background, wanted to expand her teaching certification into another area—music appreciation. A third respondent, a mechanical engineer, noted that his job required him to work with many different types of technicians, but he felt his practical knowledge in these areas was limited. This led him to take a series of practical courses in such areas as heating and air conditioning. He noted that he may some day change to a more hands-on occupation.

**Supplemental Income.** Four respondents (8 percent) returned to the community college to gain skills in order to supplement their income in an occupational area secondary to their principal jobs, although only three reported this as their primary goal. One of the four was an experienced certified public accountant, and two others had worked in several different areas during their careers. Three took courses in real estate, with one respondent earning a broker's license.

The fourth student had a ten-year career in banking, but a personal interest in food preparation led him to develop a small catering business on the side. As the business grew, the respondent started taking a variety of courses in the food and hospitality areas. Eventually this part-time pursuit may become his primary job. The respondent remarked, "I started for personal interest, but I am also interested in getting a degree in nutrition and then possibly changing careers."

**New Career.** Just over one-half of the respondents (twenty-one, or 56 percent) returned to a formal educational setting at the community college level primarily because they were seeking a new career. Several other respondents mentioned a new career as a possibility, but this was not the major reason they returned to education.

The twenty-one respondents who entered the community college with the primary goal of securing new employment can be grouped into several categories. In this chapter the sample of new-career students is divided into the following four groups: (1) no intent to relate degree and career, (2) short-time career changers, (3) job displacement new-career seekers, and (4) self-elected new beginnings.

*No Intent to Relate Degree and Career.* Three respondents reported that they never intended to use their four-year degree as educational preparation for a career. Two of them had earned a degree in the arts and never expected to earn a living in this field. One of these two respondents later completed a degree in fire science and is now an employed fireman; the other was accepted into a nursing program, but he decided not to enroll and is continuing to take community college courses for personal interest. The third respondent earned a B.S. degree in human services but never intended to work in this field. She worked in a dentist's office for four years and then enrolled in a dental hygiene program.

*Short-Time Career Changers.* Four respondents worked for a short time after graduation before they decided to change careers. Two of these respondents had earned degrees in business. One had worked for a couple of years and then started taking courses toward a degree in computer science. She stopped attending the community college after she married but is considering continuing with her studies at a later date. The other respondent had worked for short periods as a church secretary, a real estate agent, and as a postal worker. This respondent decided to pursue a career in the postal industry and is currently enrolled in a postal degree program.

Two other respondents worked for short periods in jobs directly related to their four-year degrees. One respondent with a degree in psychology worked for two years in a psychiatric hospital and is now studying to become a nurse. Another student worked as a house parent and as a director of group homes for troubled youths. This respondent was also studying to become a nurse. The last respondent in this group held a degree in theater. After working for short periods in the theater, then as a proofreader, then as a florist, this student "decided to take courses that would give me skills to get a job anywhere, since I can't always find my particular kind of work." This respondent is enrolled in a computer science program.

*Job Displacement New-Career Seekers.* Five respondents entered the community college planning to secure a new job because their current job was eliminated due to bankruptcy or industry restructuring. After receiving a B.A. in English, one respondent worked for five years for a wholesale company. When the company filed for bankruptcy, the respondent decided to make a complete change of career, enrolling in a health information program. Another respondent had worked in textile manufacturing with a background in biology. He said, "But jobs kept disappearing, so I decided to get skills in a job that hopefully wouldn't disappear. I have been taking classes one or two at a time, just to get skills. I am not sure whether I want a degree." Having earned a degree in business administration, another respondent had worked in the insurance industry, but the respondent's job was downsized. This respondent is working toward a degree in the medical assisting area.

A respondent with a degree in English worked in a bank for years. He decided to rekindle past interests that were not as yet fulfilled to help him make a decision about future career possibilities. In his words: "My division at the bank was downsized, and other banks were doing the same, so I couldn't get a job in the same line of work. I was tired of being in the bank and thought I might try something totally different. I had at one point considered going to law school, so I decided to go into the paralegal program. I also enjoyed the police aspect, so I took a lot of law enforcement courses also."

*Self-Elected New Beginnings.* Another category of respondents included seven students who were internally driven toward a new career direction. This profile is contrasted to others in which students were compelled to change by external forces. In the internally driven group, one respondent had earned degrees in elementary education and in accounting. After working as an accountant and as a bookkeeper for several years, this respondent elected to take an entirely new career direction. The respondent enrolled in and was graduated from a physical therapy program and is now working in the field. Another respondent worked for a few years in a nonprofit organization and then was employed for fifteen years in the corporate sector. His work primarily concerned computers, although his formal educational background was in counseling. He entered the community college for a completely new career: architectural drafting and interior design. A third respondent had a thirty-year career in fundraising and then decided to enroll in the community college to start a career in real estate. Another student, one with a history background, had worked for several years in jobs that required a baccalaureate degree. She then started taking courses in AutoCAD and graphics to help her husband with his business. This initial part-time pursuit has resulted in a full-time role in the business. She does not plan to complete a program but to take classes that are directly related to her work. Another respondent with a B.S. degree in commercial photography had worked for twelve years in the field and also had a background in construction. Often given photographic assignments for a civil engineering company, he leveraged this experience into a degree interest in a civil engineering program at the community college.

The last respondent in this category had a background in psychology. The respondent was a juvenile court counselor for a few years and worked for a short time in day care. The respondent said, "I thought the paralegal program would be a quick way to get a job that would pay well, and I would easily find a job." This respondent did receive a degree but now has decided to continue taking courses (now in graduate school) toward an eventual career in teaching. In going from a four-year degree to a two-year degree to graduate school, this respondent's experience counters the traditional use of different levels of higher education as a way to move up the ladder professionally.

**Personal Interest.** The nine people within the personal interest goal group divided into two major subgroups: (1) those interested in self-enrichment only and (2) those whose interests may have career implications. What distinguished these students from others taking courses for personal interest is that they had completed at least fifteen hours of credit classes; they were not occasional attendees.

*Self-Enrichment.* Six respondents took personal interest courses without any linkage to a current or future job. All six took courses in the liberal arts area. A school secretary with a background in English and Spanish took recorder classes and now plays in a musical group along with her children. An experienced computer scientist continues to take courses in photography—a long-time personal interest that, according to the respondent, "helps me to think better." A short-time teacher and long-time homemaker with an academic background in English took a variety of courses from physical activity to fine art. Finally, a bank executive "took a class with a neighbor and [has] been taking classes like oil painting and ceramics ever since." An elementary school teacher who came back to the community college for recertification also enrolled in a variety of courses from white-water canoeing to yoga, and in a similar vein an experienced nurse took several courses in ceramics and jewelry.

*Self-Enrichment–Career Linkage.* Three other respondents reported that their initial self-enrichment interest in attending the community college may lead to a career change. One experienced insurance agent with a business administration degree started taking horticultural courses with his son. He reports that he may now change to a career in horticulture upon retirement. With a background in psychology, another respondent worked a variety of jobs not related to his prior education. His interest in computers started primarily as a self-enrichment endeavor, but he now thinks he may pursue a career in this area. "I'm sort of a jack of all trades and I am trying to settle on one particular field." A final respondent, an experienced market analyst, after taking a variety of courses in nutrition and food preparation out of personal interest, was considering a career change.

## Implications

The findings of this research, coupled with findings from previous studies, suggest several major conclusions.

**Career-Related Attendance.** Like several previous studies (Renkiewicz and others, 1982; Slark, 1982; Steenhoek, 1984; Klepper, 1991; Lambert, 1993; Mattice, 1992; Trombley, 1993), this research showed that the primary reasons the PRTSs were attending the community college were career-related. Almost eight in ten respondents in this study came with career intentions—the majority (56 percent) to prepare for a new career. However, the majority of PRTSs in this study had four-year degrees in career, not liberal arts, areas. These findings dispel the belief that PRTSs are primarily liberal arts majors who could not find a job after graduating from a four-year institution. Additionally, about half the respondents had worked over five years at their jobs before returning to the community college; the average years worked for this group was sixteen. Hogan (1986) also found that many reverse transfer students were employed in professional and managerial roles prior to enrolling in the community college.

These findings may be explained by the restructuring of the American economy (Handy, 1989). The middle-level-manager sector, normally requiring a B.A. degree, has been greatly reduced in recent years. These displaced workers seek more secure jobs in the growing sectors of the economy: technical and health-related jobs. These jobs typically require more than high school but less than a four-year degree. Additionally, going up the educational hierarchy is no longer a ticket to a secure job; in fact, advanced degrees may limit prospects for employment in some areas. The notion that a higher level of education is a ladder to more money and career status has lost some of its meaning in today's workplace. Individuals are increasingly being forced to abandon the concept of their career as a vertical ascent of a single career ladder and replace it with the notion that viable careers can also be horizontal and even discontinuous (Handy, 1989). As fast-paced technological change and increased global competition continue to change the nature of jobs, it is likely that multiple careers will be increasingly commonplace. It is also likely that many individuals will interweave their careers with periods of study (Handy, 1989).

**Personal Interest Attendance.** A second finding of this study is that personal interest students made up only one-fourth of the sample. Previous research (Ross, 1982; Hogan, 1986; Kajstura, 1989) has shown that many reverse transfer students attend the community college for personal interest or self-enrichment reasons. This difference may be explained by the fact that the earlier studies did not require students to have completed at least fifteen hours to be included in the sample. It is interesting to note that the self-interest students in this study were not casual attendees. Several had completed a large number of credits, and many of the personal interest students also reported career reasons for attending but tended to be of secondary importance. Apparently, there is a group of consistent personal enrichment students, as well as a group that attends on a much more limited basis.

**Attendance by Type of PRTS.** The design of this study permitted the different types of PRTSs to emerge more fully than in prior research, which was primarily conducted with instruments based on student profiles from other populations rather than on the unique characteristics of the PRTSs. As indicated earlier, the nine prototypes identified in this study included profiles for the five identified educational goals (career exploration, skills update, income supplement, new career, and personal interest), with further breakdowns for the categories of new career and personal interest.

Regarding career exploration, this study suggests that the community college is not only a good place for traditional-age students but for individuals with considerable college and career experience who wish to explore new career options. The career update function is an expected goal for the baccalaureate reverse transfer population. The goal of income supplement for PRTSs is not surprising, given the working patterns of many Americans today. It is becoming more and more common for professionals to seek a second career on the side. Like the exploration function, this function may grow in the future.

Perhaps one of the most revealing findings of this study was the breakdown of the new-career seekers into four subgroups. Researchers previously had tended to organize these respondents into one category, but as detailed in the study, these students represent distinct groupings. Contrary to what we had anticipated, students in the first subgroup—those who never intended to use their four-year degree to secure employment—were a small part of student enrollments, fewer than 10 percent of the total, as were students in the second subgroup—those working only for a short time before deciding to return to school at the community college. For students in the third subgroup—those who enrolled at the community college after being displaced from their jobs due to external forces such as bankruptcy of their employer and industry restructuring—it is not clear why these respondents did not seek to continue their education at the graduate level. Almost 20 percent of the respondents were in the fourth subgroup—those who returned to education because they were primarily driven by internal, personal motivation to change their careers.

## Conclusion

The postbaccalaureate reverse transfer student represents a very different type of second-chance student for the community college. For these students, the label "second chance" has lost much of its original meaning. The study's results have helped dispel the long-accepted notion that a higher level of education is an automatic ladder to more money and career status. Changes in our society and the increasing value of life-long education suggest that educational consumers throughout their lifetimes will return to various types of educational institutions to meet their personal and career circumstances. PRTSs are not going down a level of education; they are going to the right level of education.

Given the size and the unique nature of the PRTS population, continued response to the needs of these students may lead to the creation of a distinct new mission area for the community college in the near future. Certainly, this student population will compel educators to develop new strategies for recruitment, academic support, and instruction. Growing recognition of this population will also redefine the mission of the community college to key constituency groups and the public.

Understanding more about this population will help prepare community colleges for this eventuality. This study has broadened our understanding, but the results now need to be further substantiated and additional research questions identified in this study need to be asked. A comprehensive, national study is long overdue.

## References

Handy, C. *The Age of Unreason.* Boston: Harvard Business School Press, 1989.

Hogan, R. R. "An Update on Reverse Transfers to Two-Year Colleges." *Community/Junior College Quarterly,* 1986, *10,* 295–306.

Kajstura, A. "Reverse Transfer Students in Illinois Community Colleges." Unpublished doctoral dissertation, Southern Illinois University at Carbondale, 1989.

Klepper, D. F. "A Descriptive Analysis of Completer Transfer Students at a Virginia Community College." Doctoral dissertation, University of Virginia, 1991. *Dissertation Abstracts International, 51,* 4002A.

Lambert, R. J. "College-wide: Post-baccalaureate Reverse Transfer Students Attending Baltimore Community Colleges." Unpublished doctoral dissertation, University of Maryland, College Park, 1993.

Mattice, N. J. "Students with Baccalaureate Degrees, Fall 1992." Valencia, Calif.: College of the Canyons, 1992.

Renkiewicz, N. K., Hirsch, P. M., Drummond, M. E., and Mitchell, G. N. *The Reverse Transfer Student: An Emerging Population.* Sacramento: Northern California Community College Research Groups, Los Rios Community College, 1982. (ED 223 3081)

Ross, R. A. "The Reverse Transfer Phenomenon at Piedmont Virginia Community College, Fall Quarter, 1981." Charlottesville: Piedmont Virginia Community College, 1982.

Slark, J. "Reverse Transfer Student Study." Santa Ana, Calif.: Santa Ana College, 1982.

Steenhoek, A. C. "The Reverse Transfer Student and Comparisons of the Reverse Transfer Student to the Lateral Transfer Student, and the Native Student at Cerritos College." Doctoral dissertation, University of La Verne, 1984. *Dissertation Abstracts International, 46,* 2172A.

Trombley, W. H. *Public Policy by Anecdote: The Case of Community College Fees.* San Jose: California Higher Education Policy Center, 1993. (ED 356 806)

*JOHN W. QUINLEY is director of research and analysis for the College and University Personnel Association. He is also the former director of planning and research for Central Piedmont Community College, Charlotte, North Carolina.*

*MELISSA P. QUINLEY is associate professor of mathematics at Montgomery College, Montgomery County, Maryland. She has twenty years of experience as a mathematics instructor, primarily in the community college setting.*

*A study of undergraduate reverse transfers in an urban environment indicates some complex patterns of institutional attendance and implies that the community college plays multiple roles in the lives of those beginning their postsecondary education in a four-year institution.*

# Reverse Transfer Students in an Urban Postsecondary System in Oregon

*Susan K. Bach, Melissa A. Banks, David K. Blanchard, Mary K. Kinnick, Mary F. Ricks, Juliette M. Stoering*

In 1990 the final report of the [Oregon] Governor's Commission on Higher Education in the Portland Metropolitan Area recommended implementing programs that "link students so they can transfer smoothly from high schools to community colleges and then to Portland State or other institutions" (1990, p. 45). More specifically, programs were to be developed to help students transfer easily to the university from the three public community colleges in Portland's urban area: Clackamas Community College, Portland Community College, and Mt. Hood Community College.

As part of this effort, the Portland State University/Community College Research Consortium (CRC) was formed in 1992 to "conduct research designed to strengthen the transfer role of the [Portland] metropolitan community colleges and the transfer process such that student educational success is enhanced" (Kinnick, 1994, p. 3). The research agenda of the CRC was initially shaped by and continues to be shaped by local institutional leaders.

The consortium recently conducted a study that identified four distinct patterns of undergraduate student attendance in Portland's Urban Postsecondary System (UPS), defined as the three local community colleges and Portland State University (Bach and others, 1998). These four patterns are defined as (1) True Linear Urban Transfer Students (T-LURTSs)—those who follow a traditional linear transfer pattern within the UPS, (2) False Linear Urban Transfer Students (F-LURTSs)—those who are linear transfers but have some postsecondary experience outside the UPS, (3) Complex Urban Transfer Students-Community College (CURT-Cs)—those with more complex patterns who first entered the UPS through a community college, and

(4) Complex Urban Transfer Students-University (CURT-Us)—those with a more complex pattern who first entered the UPS through the university (Bach and others, 1998).

Each of the four UPS institutions is located within reasonable commuting distance in the Portland metropolitan area. Only about one-third of the students in the study followed the pattern of a direct path from high school to the community college and then on to the university (T-LURTSs). Nearly one-fourth of the students entered the UPS at the university level rather than through one of the community colleges. This was the pattern labeled CURT-Us. The majority of student enrollment patterns provided strong evidence of the transfer "swirl" identified by de los Santos and Wright (1990). These patterns suggest that framing "student transfer" as linear and one-way (from the two-year college to the four-year college) fails to account for the attendance patterns of significant numbers of students in an urban postsecondary system.

In this chapter we will examine a subset of CURT-Us—students who left the university to attend the community college. Our goal was to understand more about why these students left the university, the role of the community college in their education, and their subsequent postsecondary attendance.

## Methods

The original study (Bach and others, 1998) consisted of a sample of community college students who completed at least three credits at one of the three community colleges in the UPS in 1990–91, did not return to the same community college in the following year, and had a record of enrollment at the UPS university. University enrollment included any term before, after, or concurrent with the 1990–91 enrollment at the community college. University records used were current through spring term, 1995; degree information was current through spring term, 1996. For the reverse transfer study undertaken here, degree information was updated through summer 1998.

From the original population of 5,057 students, a stratified random sample of 504 students was selected. Detailed data were analyzed for a subset of 336 students who were undergraduates at their first UPS university enrollment and who were not concurrently enrolled at a community college during their first term of attendance at the university. Analyses showed that students fell into forty-eight discrete attendance patterns, with 23 percent ($N = 77$) beginning in the UPS university. These seventy-seven students were the CURT-U students we are examining in this chapter.

This initial study looked only at patterns of attendance among the four institutions in the UPS and documented a conservative profile of student enrollment behavior. For the current study, we expanded the coding structure for the seventy-seven CURT-Us to include all other two- and four-year public and private institutions attended by students. This enhanced view of attendance patterns revealed several individuals whose initial postsecondary attendance was at a two-year institution, and they were removed from the sample. We also identified two students who remained continuously enrolled at a four-year institution and concurrently enrolled at some point at a community college. Because they did not ever leave the university sector, we removed them from the sample as well. The remaining sixty-one students, the redefined CURT-U group, were identified as "true" undergraduate reverse transfers, that is, those whose initial postsecondary enrollment was at a four-year institution and who later transferred to a two-year institution before completing a baccalaureate degree.

Three members of the CRC research team examined these students' transcripts to construct a narrative summary of each student's educational career and to generate a set of observations, including a set of "themes" about the roles played by the community college in these students' education. We noted (1) the number of times a student "switched" institutions, (2) any incidence(s) of concurrent enrollment, (3) the number of different institutions attended, and (4) the pattern of reverse transfer (where "single" = university to community college only; "double" = university to community college to university; and "multiple" = university to community college to university to community college, and so on).

Several study limitations must be noted. The student sample for the original study required that a student attend both the UPS university and at least one of the three UPS community colleges at some time. As a result, findings may not generalize to studies that define their sample differently. Also, our data source was restricted to student transcripts. This information allowed us to describe accurately and in detail student attendance behavior. Without information collected directly from the students, however, in some cases we could only speculate about their reasons for leaving the university and the roles of the community college in their lives. Also, baccalaureate degree achievement rates are conservative because they include only records from the UPS university, and it is possible that students earned baccalaureate degrees at other institutions.

Finally, we defined *reverse transfer* in very broad terms. In a number of instances, students were included in the CURT-U group solely on the basis of credits earned prior to graduation from high school. Transcript data could not tell us, however, if individuals earned these credits by taking courses on-site at the university, by taking courses at the high school, which were transcripted by the university, or through College-Level Examination Program (CLEP) exams at the high school and receiving university credit. As a result, and to provide as complete a picture as possible of a student's postsecondary experience, we chose to leave them in our study. The incidence of "early credit" we observed, however, raises the issue of how to consider advanced placement and other credits earned prior to high school graduation when studying reverse transfers.

## Findings

The sixty-one students identified for this study included thirty-one females and thirty males; eleven were minority students, predominately Asian American. Although the current age of individuals in the study ranged from twenty-five to fifty-four, 87.3 percent had entered postsecondary education for the first time at age seventeen, eighteen, or nineteen, and the remaining eight students were between the ages of twenty-one to twenty-seven at first enrollment.

By definition, all students in this sample began their postsecondary careers at a four-year institution. Based on transcript records of academic history through spring 1995, the UPS university was also an end point for the majority of students (77.0 percent). The remaining students either completed or terminated enrollment at a community college or were concurrently enrolled in both sectors. More than half (52.5 percent) of the sixty-one students attended only the four UPS institutions; most students attending schools outside the UPS were enrolled at four-year institutions. Concurrent enrollment was a common occurrence, with twenty-two (36 percent) students attending more than one institution concurrently at some point during their academic careers. Most concurrent enrollment involved attendance at the four UPS institutions.

Analysis of the students' detailed enrollment history revealed that twenty-four students (39.3 percent) attended only two institutions, moving back and forth between the UPS university and a single UPS community college. Twenty-seven students (44.3 percent) attended three institutions; the remaining ten (16 percent) attended a maximum of either four or five different institutions. Within this framework, patterns of enrollment varied greatly, and we identified forty-nine discrete attendance patterns characterized by multiple moves among institutions. The range of moves for all students was 1 to 11, with an average of 4.3 moves (see Table 5.1).

Results differed to some extent by gender. The range of moves among institutions for males was 1 to 8 with a mean of 3.6 moves; numbers were significantly higher for females with a range of 1 to 11 moves and an average of 4.9 moves. Females in this study were three times more likely than males to make more than 6 moves.

Focusing on reverse transfer from the university to the community college revealed that only five students made a single reverse (movement from

### Table 5.1. Enrollment Patterns and Reverse Transfer

|  | Number of Moves | | | Reverse Transfer | | |
|  | N | Range | Mean | Single | Double | Multiple |
|---|---|---|---|---|---|---|
| All cases | 61 | 1–11 | 4.3 | 5 | 34 | 22 |
| Females | 31 | 1–11 | 4.9* | 1 | 15 | 15 |
| Males | 30 | 1–8 | 3.6 | 4 | 19 | 7 |

*$t = -2.36, p < .022$

four-year to two-year sector). More than half (55.7 percent) made double reverses (movement from four-year to two-year sector and back to the four-year sector), and many of these were characterized by complex sequential enrollment at either one or more four-year institutions or one or more two-year schools. Approximately one-third of the students made multiple reverses from university to community college to university to community college, and so on. Again, differences were noted based on gender (see Table 5.1). Almost two-thirds of the males made double reverse transfers, compared to slightly less than half the female students; twice as many females as males were classified as multiple reverse transfers.

The point at which students first transferred from four-year to two-year institutions varied considerably. Eleven students (18.0 percent) exited initially at the end of their first term. Incidence of first transfer for the remaining students was somewhat evenly distributed among those who exited after two or three terms (29.5 percent), after four to six terms (27.9 percent), and after seven or more terms (24.6 percent). Data indicate that males were more likely than females to break from the four-year sector within the first six terms of enrollment. Students identified as being in academic distress were more likely to leave the university after two or three terms (35.7 percent) rather than after their initial term of enrollment (10.7 percent), while approximately one-fourth (24.2 percent) of those not in academic distress made the move to a community college after only one term of enrollment at a four-year institution.

On average, students earned approximately one-third of their total credits at a community college. Community college transcripts revealed that forty-one students (67.2 percent) enrolled in a clearly identifiable pattern of lower-division transfer course work, some in combination with developmental skills or career guidance courses. Another thirteen (21.3 percent) enrolled in a combination of transfer and vocational curricula, with many of the latter serving as transferable courses as well. Of the remaining students, five enrolled at the community college in vocational programs and two others in course work unrelated to baccalaureate degree attainment.

By spring 1998, thirty-six students in the sample (59.0 percent) had completed baccalaureate degrees at the UPS university. Thirteen students also had completed community college degrees or certificates, twelve at UPS institutions. Rates of baccalaureate completion were only slightly higher for associate degree completers (61.5 percent) than for noncompleters (58.3 percent). Many students persisted to the baccalaureate degree over extended periods of time, with a range of 4 to 29 years and a mean of 10.7 years. Differences by gender are noted in range and average time to degree completion, with higher numbers for females (see Table 5.2). Only one student out of the thirty-six completed a baccalaureate degree within four years. Eleven students (30.6 percent) completed within six years, and an additional eleven students (30.6 percent) completed in seven to ten years. The remaining thirteen students (36.1 percent) completed degrees in more than ten years; five of these individuals, all females, completed in more than twenty years.

#### Table 5.2.  Degree Completion and Time to Degree

| | Students Who Complete | | Years to B.A. or B.S. | |
|---|---|---|---|---|
| | CC Degree | B.A. or B.S. | Range | Mean |
| All cases | 13 | 36 | 4–29 | 10.7 |
| Females | 6 | 19 | 5–29 | 13.2* |
| Males | 7 | 17 | 4–15 | 8.2 |

$*t = -2.38, p < .025$

## Role of the Community College in UPS Students' Reverse Transfer

Several distinct themes were identified regarding the role of the community college in the reverse transfer process. Because our sample size was small and we were limited to inferring the use of the community college from transcript data only, we did not attempt to quantify the themes. Instead, we approximated the proportion of students in each of these broad categories.

**Academic Difficulty.** Approximately two out of five students experienced academic distress at the university, based either on evidence of formal academic warning, academic disqualification, or a recognizable pattern of difficulty with course work (repeated course failure or low GPA).

We further divided this group of students into two subgroups. In one group a substantial number of students used the community college to effect a successful academic turnaround and subsequently returned to the university. More than half of these students completed baccalaureate degrees. Students in this group made extensive use of the community college; most earned at least thirty-one credits, and more than half earned sixty-one or more credits. A second group in academic difficulty at the university achieved only limited academic success after attending a community college. Students in the latter group were less engaged at the community college, with most earning fewer than forty credit hours, and they typically did not complete baccalaureate degrees. Transcript records revealed that many of the students in academic distress experienced difficulty with college mathematics courses and other math-related curricula (science, economics, engineering, and business) and used the community college either to build prerequisite skills or to improve performance (and GPA) in these subjects.

A third, related subgroup of cases was identified as false-start–restart students. Rather than earning poor grades, these individuals demonstrated a pattern over several terms of exiting the university without successfully completing any course work. They repeatedly enrolled in classes but left (either by formal course withdrawal or informally with no basis for a grade) for unknown reasons. However, after subsequent enrollment at a community college, many returned to the university and completed baccalaureate degrees.

**Opportunity.** Approximately one-third of the students did not demonstrate academic distress at the university. Rather, they appeared to use the community college primarily to supplement their work at the university, enrolling in developmental skills courses, taking selected prerequisite courses, or completing either substantial portions of lower-division requirements or all general education lower-division requirements, the latter of which constitutes a block transfer degree. Their choice of courses appeared to be deliberate and focused on the goal of attaining a baccalaureate degree. Students in the opportunity group also fell into two distinct subgroups: (1) those who used the community college to fill in their university course work (enrolled for thirty or fewer credits) by taking a limited number of specific transfer courses and (2) those who made substantial use of the community college to complete baccalaureate degree requirements. Many of the latter enrolled for more than sixty credits. In addition to lower-division transfer courses, these students took a variety of professional technical courses, particularly in business but also in other fields, that enabled them to earn associate of applied science degrees or certificates, as well as transfer credits to the university. Approximately 70 percent of these students attained a baccalaureate degree.

We also identified as opportunity students those who earned university credit while still in high school, a situation that served to jump-start their postsecondary careers. Two-thirds of these students were also identified as those who used the community college to supplement their baccalaureate course taking, and several also earned early credits through the community college.

**Other.** The remaining students (approximately one out of five) appeared to use the community college to explore career and other life options (evidenced by concentrations of course work in multiple fields), achieve specific short-term employment objectives, and pursue avocational or personal interests apparently unrelated to degree attainment. Their involvement at the community college was more limited, with many students earning fewer than fifteen credits; fewer than half of these students earned baccalaureate degrees.

## Conclusions

We derived the following conclusions from these data:

*Few students made a single reverse from university to community college.* Most made double or multiple reverses back and forth between the two sectors. Moreover, students didn't just move from one university to a single community college and then back again. They moved from one university to another university before enrolling at a community college, and then moved among several community colleges before returning to the university.

*Students were highly mobile.* They moved freely and frequently among both UPS and non-UPS institutions. Although as a group they attended a variety of two- and four-year schools, enrollment patterns for individual students typically involved a limited number of different institutions.

*Students in this group were very persistent.* Although some of the students finished the baccalaureate in fewer than six years, most took more than seven years from time of first postsecondary enrollment to completion of a B.A. or B.S. degree.

*There were gender differences both in attendance pattern and time to degree.* Women were more mobile, making more moves among institutions than the men. Many women also took substantially longer than their male counterparts to complete baccalaureate degrees, with several persisting for more than two decades.

*Students appeared to use the community college for different purposes at different points in their educational careers and sometimes for multiple purposes at the same time.* The community college played an important role in helping many students who experienced academic difficulty at the four-year institution return to this sector better prepared to succeed. For a number of students who tried the university but left before establishing an academic record, the community college became a place to successfully restart their postsecondary careers. For many students the community college served as a place to complete a substantial portion of lower-division transfer course work to supplement their enrollment at a university.

*A significant number of students experienced difficulty with university mathematics or with university courses that required a strong mathematics background.* For many of these students the community college was a place to strengthen their mathematics proficiency or to consider program and career options that required less mathematics.

*A sizeable number of students earned college credit prior to graduation from high school.* This may be a phenomenon of an urban environment where universities and community colleges can identify specific feeder high schools and develop articulation agreements that facilitate jump-starting the postsecondary experience.

## Implications

Students appeared to use the UPS as a system, availing themselves of educational resources when and where they needed them. In this regard, students appeared to be opportunistic and to use available educational resources to good advantage. We speculate that many students enrolled at the two-year school for reasons of cost and convenience: low tuition, locations close to home or work, and classes scheduled at times suited to personal schedules. Transcript data, however, could not confirm this speculation.

Their use patterns lend credence to current efforts by the UPS institutions to collaborate in developing policies (such as dual admission) and in providing programs and services to meet the needs of these students. These efforts include exploring ways to share student records to support a coordinated system of student advising and to view students as "our" students within the system. Student and academic support services are needed that serve part-time and working students as well as those who begin, leave the system, and then return to restart their educational careers. Providers of these services should consider the possibility that the needs of women and men may differ.

A number of students experienced academic difficulty at the four-year institution. Some of these difficulties related to mathematics and to fields of study that require mathematics. The good news is that many of the students, with support from the community college, were able to make a turnaround. The challenge, however, is to address the factors contributing to the initial academic difficulty. These factors may include the level of precollege mathematics preparation, precollege advising regarding college choice, assessment information used in admissions and course placement decisions, career advising, program and course advising, and the form in and speed at which the university intervenes when a student is in academic difficulty. The Oregon University System is developing the Proficiency-Based Admission Standards System (PASS) to provide more detailed information about what a student knows and can do by complementing the current system that relies heavily on high school grades. PASS has the potential for providing students, support staff, and faculty in schools and colleges with better information for making educational choices.

The findings also have implications for how we assess the effectiveness of our institutions. Use of measures such as time to degree and transfer rates appears problematic when assessing community college effectiveness. These measures are of limited value in helping us describe outcomes related to completion of educational goals. Clearly, a long-term perspective is needed in order to assess student achievement of the baccalaureate degree and to observe the ways and the times at which students use educational resources to support their needs and aspirations.

Future research needs to examine how reverse transfer in urban environments compares to that in nonurban environments. For instance, how does the availability of local educational resources affect student attendance patterns, the ways students use these resources, and their completion of the baccalaureate degree? We suspect that the students in this study may be more mobile and able to complete degrees because of their location in an area rich with postsecondary institutions and with institutions that have strong articulation agreements and some history of collaboration.

Finally, we are led to conclude that several constructs used to consider the student transfer process are problematic. Viewing the attendance patterns of transfer students as a swirl seems somewhat misleading because the term *swirl* suggests a lack of focus and the absence of intention. Most students in this study appeared to be both focused and purposeful, as other researchers of multiple transfer patterns have found (for example, Adelman, 1992; Kearney, Townsend, and Kearney, 1995). They use educational resources at times and places and for purposes that fit their circumstances and that can advance their learning and their goals. The term *reverse transfer* may also be misleading. It suggests that students move to the community college from the four-year institution and end their careers there. In fact, only a few students in this study fit this description. Most returned to the four-year sector, following diverse attendance patterns over an extended period of time. *Reverse* also implies that a student moves backward. This study suggests that the movement is always forward. Over the course of the study, we have come to appreciate the efforts many of these students continue to demonstrate in pursuit of an education.

## References

Adelman, C. *The Way We Are: The Community College as American Thermometer.* Washington, D.C.: U.S. Department of Education, 1992. (ED 338 269)

Bach, S., Banks, M., Kinnick, M., Ricks, M., Stoering, J., and Walleri, D. "Student Attendance Patterns and Performance in an Urban Postsecondary Environment." Paper presented at the Thirty-Seventh Annual Forum of the Association for Institutional Research, Minneapolis, May 20, 1998.

de los Santos, A., and Wright, I. "Maricopa's Swirling Students." *Community, Technical and Junior College Journal,* June/July 1990, pp. 32–34.

Governor's Commission on Higher Education in the Metropolitan Area. "Working Together: A Community and Academic Partnership for Greater Portland." Salem, Ore.: Office of the Governor, 1990.

Kearney, G., Townsend, B., and Kearney, T. "Multiple Transfer Students in a Public Urban University: Background Characteristics and Interinstitutional Movements." *Research in Higher Education,* 1995, 36 (3), 323–344.

Kinnick, M. "Portland State University/Community College Research Consortium Report." Unpublished report, School of Education, Portland State University, Portland, Oregon, 1994.

*SUSAN K. BACH is director of institutional research, Portland Community College, Portland, Oregon.*

*MELISSA A. BANKS is research coordinator, Clackamas Community College, Oregon City, Oregon.*

*DAVID K. BLANCHARD is research associate, Mt. Hood Community College, Gresham, Oregon.*

*MARY K. KINNICK is professor of education, Graduate School of Education, Portland State University, Portland, Oregon.*

*MARY F. RICKS is research associate professor emerita, Portland State University, Portland, Oregon.*

*JULIETTE M. STOERING is research associate, Office of Institutional Research and Planning, Portland State University, Portland, Oregon.*

*This chapter details the results of a study of postbaccalaureate reverse transfers attending community colleges in Missouri.*

# Bachelor's Degree Students Attending Community Colleges: A Look at Postbaccalaureate Reverse Transfers in Missouri

*Terry L. Barnes, Laura M. Robinson*

The transfer function has always been a primary focus of community colleges. Although this still holds true today, transfer students are not the same students they were even fifteen years ago. The community college transfer student of the past was a student who entered a two-year college after high school, enrolled in a "university-transfer," associate-of-arts-degree, sixty-four–credit-hour articulated program. On completion of the program, the student "transferred" to a four-year college or university.

Another group of transfer students that has emerged is the undergraduate student who matriculates at a four-year school and then "reverse transfers" to the community college at least once before returning to the four-year institution to earn a bachelor's degree. These two types of transfer students represent a linear model of transfer, the paradigm that has guided most of the conversations and public policy decisions surrounding transfer and articulation among community colleges and four-year institutions.

This paradigm for thinking about transferability of credits among and between two-year and four-year colleges is being challenged by another type of transfer student—the student who attends a community college after obtaining a bachelor's degree from a four-year institution. In this chapter we will describe the results of a study developed to examine this type of transfer student—the postbaccalaureate reverse transfer student (PRTSs)—in Missouri. Specifically, we sought to determine the nature and extent of mobility among Missouri's recent public four-year college graduates who subsequently enrolled in community college courses and programs in Missouri. Additionally, we surveyed chief academic officers of Missouri public community colleges about their perceptions of this phenomenon in order to compare and contrast human viewpoints with actual enrollment data.

## Investigating Missouri's Movement of Postbaccalaureate Student Transfer to Community Colleges

The Missouri Coordinating Board for Higher Education (CBHE) provides leadership and vision for Missouri's systems of four-year and two-year public and private institutions. On a semester basis, each public institution provides the CBHE data and information from their enrollment records. Semester records from each institution are gathered through the Missouri Student Achievement Survey (MSAS) and stored for CBHE research and analysis.

In 1998, the Missouri system of public community colleges included twelve public, tax-supported districts with seventeen campuses. The community college taxing districts are part and parcel of twelve nonstatutory geographic service regions that are somewhat equally dispersed throughout the state. In fall 1997, the community colleges reported an enrollment of 71,999 credit students.

The Missouri higher education system also includes nine public baccalaureate colleges and universities, as well as four campuses of the University of Missouri System. These institutions combined enrolled nearly 100,000 undergraduate credit students in the same year (Missouri Coordinating Board for Higher Education, 1998).

In the fall of 1998, we used the MSAS records from all public two-year and four-year institutions to develop an initial profile of public institutions' baccalaureate degree graduates who later enroll in Missouri public community colleges. We identified and tracked Missouri bachelor's degree graduates from public baccalaureate institutions from five graduation dates: 1991–92, 1992–93, 1993–94, 1994–95, and 1995–96.

Next we tracked each cohort of bachelor's degree graduates to determine to what extent its members subsequently enrolled in a Missouri public community college. The 1991–92 bachelor's degree graduates were tracked for five years to see whether enrollment took place in a Missouri community college any time before spring semester 1998. The 1992–93 bachelor's graduates were tracked for four years, until spring 1998; the 1993–94 graduates for three years; the 1994–95 graduates for two years; and the 1995–96 graduates for one year. Trends were analyzed to determine whether the attendance patterns of bachelor's degree graduates who later enroll in community colleges are on the rise.

During the fall of 1998, each of the chief academic officers of the twelve Missouri public community colleges was invited to participate in individual e-mail interviews. Eight completed a researcher-designed survey consisting of five open-ended questions created to aid the researchers in learning how the community college chief academic officers describe the nature and extent of the postbaccalaureate reverse transfer phenomenon. The five survey questions were:

1. Do you think your institution has a sizeable number of bachelor's degree reverse-transferring students currently enrolled at your college?
2. Do you think the number of bachelor's degree reverse-transferring students has experienced an upward trend over the last five years?
3. Do you think the enrollment increases, if any, among bachelor's degree reverse-transferring students is becoming a significant market niche for your college?
4. What are the primary reasons given for bachelor's degree reverse-transferring students enrolling at your college?
5. Do you think that most of the bachelor's degree graduates attend part-time rather than full-time?

We acknowledge that the generalizability of the survey findings is limited. There is no assurance that the attendance patterns, as perceived by the chief academic officers of community colleges, actually match those of bachelor's degree reverse-transferring students who were not surveyed. However, our interest was in learning how the officers perceived the phenomenon of baccalaureate degree holders attending community colleges, including why these students return to community colleges.

## Enrollment Profile of Bachelor's Degree Graduates

Data from the 1998 Missouri Student Achievement Survey were the most recent data available at the time of this writing. These data provided two-year college enrollment profiles for bachelor's degree graduates over a five-year time period—1991 to 1996. The profiles illustrate the relationship between length of time from graduation at one of Missouri's public four-year schools to enrollment in one of Missouri's public community colleges.

*1991–92 bachelor's degree graduates.* At the end of the 1991–92 academic year, Missouri public four-year institutions produced a total of 7,721 baccalaureate degree graduates. By the end of fall semester, 1997, or within five years of graduation, 406 (5.25 percent) had enrolled in a Missouri public community college. Of these students, 71 percent had enrolled within the first three years after graduation.

*1992–93 bachelor's degree graduates.* At the end of the 1992–93 academic year, Missouri public four-year institutions produced a total of 9,608 baccalaureate degree graduates. By the end of fall semester of 1997, or within four years after graduation, 481 (5.00 percent) had enrolled in a Missouri public community college. Seventy-nine percent of the 481 had enrolled within the first three years after graduation.

*1993–94 bachelor's degree graduates.* At the end of the 1993–94 academic year, Missouri public four-year institutions produced a total of 10,369 baccalaureate degree graduates. By the end of fall semester of 1997, or within three years after graduation, 449 (4.33 percent) had enrolled in a Missouri public community college.

*1994–95 bachelor's degree graduates.* At the end of the 1994–95 academic year, Missouri public four-year institutions produced a total of 15,416 baccalaureate degree graduates. By the end of fall semester of 1997, or within two years after graduation, 433 (2.80 percent) had enrolled in a Missouri public community college.

*1995–96 bachelor's degree graduates.* At the end of the 1995–96 academic year, Missouri public four-year institutions produced a total of 14,647 baccalaureate degree graduates. By the end of fall semester of 1997, or within one year after graduation, 235 (1.60 percent) had enrolled in a Missouri public community college.

Table 6.1 indicates the numeric growth of PRTSs in Missouri public community colleges. The increase from 1993–94 to 1994–95 as well as from 1994–95 to 1995–96 was particularly great, with PRTSs' enrollment averaging 26 percent growth during each of those years. However, these findings need to be considered in light of the overall trend of increasing bachelor's degree graduates at Missouri's public four-year institutions. During these five years, the number of graduates nearly doubled, from 7,721 to 14,647. Table 6.2 reports how the percentage of PRTSs enrolling in Missouri community colleges remained steady in the face of such remarkable growth in the four-year sector.

Table 6.3 compares the extent to which students with previously earned bachelor's degrees chose to enroll at an urban or rural community college. These data indicate that students with baccalaureate degrees enrolled in urban community colleges, as compared to rural community colleges, by nearly four to one.

**Table 6.1. Bachelor's Degree Graduates Enrolled at Missouri Community Colleges Within One Year After Graduation**

| Year Graduated with Bachelor's Degree | Year First Enrolled at Community College | Number Enrolled |
|---|---|---|
| 1991–92 | 1992–93 | 160 |
| 1992–93 | 1993–94 | 165 |
| 1993–94 | 1994–95 | 205 |
| 1994–95 | 1995–96 | 260 |
| 1995–96 | 1996–97 | 235 |

**Table 6.2.  Missouri Community College Enrollment as a
Percentage of Bachelor's Degree Graduates**

| Academic Year | Number of Bachelor's Degree Graduates* | Percentage Enrolled at Community College Within Next Academic Year |
|---|---|---|
| 1991–92 | 7,721 | 2.1 |
| 1992–93 | 9,608 | 1.7 |
| 1993–94 | 10,369 | 2.0 |
| 1994–95 | 15,416 | 1.7 |
| 1995–96 | 14,647 | 1.6 |

* From Missouri public four-year institutions.

**Table 6.3.  Urban Versus Rural Enrollment at Community
Colleges by Percentage**

| Year First Enrolled at Community College | Percentage Enrolled at Urban Community College | Percentage Enrolled at Rural Community College |
|---|---|---|
| 1992–93 | 83.0 | 17.0 |
| 1993–94 | 81.9 | 19.1 |
| 1994–95 | 78.3 | 21.7 |
| 1995–96 | 81.5 | 18.5 |
| 1996–97 | 75.7 | 24.3 |

## Interview Findings

Supplementing the data showing enrollment trends are perceptions of the chief
academic officers (CAOs) of Missouri's community colleges. According to their
responses to an e-mail survey, the CAOs believed that a sizeable number of
bachelor's degree students reverse transfer back to the community college.
Although the CAOs were not asked to provide official numbers or give any ref-
erence points, it is interesting to note that most respondents perceived the
community colleges to have more bachelor's degree students enrolled than the
CBHE database recorded. One CAO wrote that some campus officials estimate
that bachelor's degree reverse transfers equal or even exceed the number who
transfer from the community college to universities and complete bachelor's
degrees. Other CAOs believed the numbers of PRTSs are increasing on a yearly
basis. However, most agreed that the numbers, as a percentage of total credit
enrollments, are small and not a significant market niche.

The CAOs typically perceived that most of the PRTSs were enrolling in technical programs and courses. One institution that tracks these students indicated
that 78 percent of them are enrolled in technical programs. When asked about
the primary reasons why students with bachelor's degrees subsequently enroll at
the community college, most of the respondents indicated that taking computer
courses, upgrading skills for a current job, or planning to completely change pro-
fessions were the primary reasons. One respondent suggested that PRTSs could
look forward to relatively high-paying and readily available jobs after rather short

periods of study at the community college, such as training in telecommunications, IBM AS400 mainframe computer, or networking certification.

When asked about PRTSs' enrollment patterns, most CAOs agree that these students are attending predominantly part-time. There was, however, no clear agreement among CAOs regarding the extent to which these students are daytime or evening students.

## Discussion

A robust economy and statewide postsecondary workforce development initiatives may be contributing to shifts in college student transfer patterns, especially among community colleges. Community colleges seem to be realizing yet another comparative advantage over four-year institutions. In Missouri, a rather small but enduring number of recent four-year college graduates opt for additional specialized training and education at the community college over traditional graduate school work. It can be concluded that the community college sector has discovered and benefited from a relatively unknown market niche—the recent bachelor's degree graduate. This study suggests that about 5 percent of the annual baccalaureate degree graduates from Missouri public four-year institutions enroll later at a Missouri community college. From these figures, it is projected annually that nearly one thousand bachelor's degree holders ultimately enroll in Missouri community colleges in credit programs and courses.

Future research will be needed to determine whether this new transfer pattern has evolved more from changes in the economy and personal work requirements or from community college marketing or promotional strategies. Readers and researchers are encouraged to replicate this modest investigation again in Missouri and in other states. There is need for continued longitudinal investigations of student attendance patterns, particularly of students who have earned a bachelor's degree and wish to return to the community college for more education and training. Additional research should be targeted specifically at identifying unique characteristics that best describe the bachelor's degree recipients who choose to enroll in community colleges after graduation rather than enter the labor market exclusively or commence work on a master's degree.

Further investigation should focus on bachelor's degree recipients' age, gender, major at the baccalaureate institution, GPA, and location of the bachelor's degree granting institution. Other important attributes to analyze are satisfaction with the chosen bachelor's degree major and career goals, differentiation between major and field of work, and perceptions of changing opportunities and risks within the world of work.

The interviews with the chief academic officers of the community colleges served to identify several other areas of focus. It is intriguing that, given all the educational choices available to baccalaureate degree holders, some students forego graduate school and invest in formal or informal training at a community college. Traditional assumptions about a continuity of students' educational goals after graduating with a bachelor's degree need to be balanced with new questions about discontinuities. These students may be seeing themselves not as reverse-transferring to a community college but as advancing or redirecting career choices. These students may not see the postsecondary system in terms of "feeder" and "receiver" institutions. It is more likely that the students see themselves as the customers of one institution at a time and enroll for specific, anticipated returns on their investment of time and money. Future analysis will be needed to determine if this new transfer pattern has evolved more from change in the economy and personal work requirements than from community college marketing or promotional strategies.

A key question in this area is why bachelor's degree students are enrolling in community colleges. Possible hypotheses range from changing careers to upgrading skills, to seeking better pay or promotional opportunities related to a current job, to getting retrained because the bachelor's degree major did not produce a suitable job, or getting new skills because of an employment layoff. Because one could hypothesize that recent bachelor's degree students attend community colleges for pragmatic reasons, it would be helpful to identify the types of courses or programs being taken. Questions about educational intent should be pursued. For example, are students enrolled for associate degree, certificate, or nondegree purposes? Future research needs to examine the hypothesis that bachelor's degree students enroll in community colleges to earn new technical or applied skills that are not taught in universities. It would be helpful to compare the bachelor's degree major to the program or course of study undertaken at the community college.

Additional research should probe the extent to which these students are currently employed on a full- or part-time basis and enrolled on a full- or part-time basis. The amount of elapsed time between graduating with a bachelor's degree and later enrolling in a community college would be useful information to know as well. A final area involves the bachelor's degree students' attitudes toward the community college learning environment and its payoff toward achieving new or modified career goals.

## Implications

This study assists in the generation of a more accurate profile of the nature and extent of postbaccalaureate reverse transfers, if only in the state of Missouri. These informal data add to the existing information on the characteristics of Missouri traditional transfer, traditional reverse transfer, and now the transitioning bachelor's degree graduate who learns additional skills at the community college.

A variety of implications are inherent in a conversation about reverse transfer students, especially when considering the definition of *transfer* that incorporates the concept of bachelor's degree students enrolling later in a community college. Specifically, there are implications for an examination of the entire community college transfer function, the generation of a community college reverse transfer student profile, the study of the changes to the community college culture, and the validation of public policies related to statewide workforce development, training, and education initiatives.

This study has significant implications for understanding the phenomenon of postbaccalaureate reverse transfer students. Acknowledging this new type of student helps formulate a more accurate picture of the institution's transfer function and indeed may require a more accurate definition of this unique type of transfer student. Although inconsistencies in defining *transfer student* are evident, no one questions that the term typically means progressing from a "lower-division" institution to an "upper-division" institution. Some four-year institutions and community colleges are not appropriately prepared to account for the traditional reverse transfer student, as their tracking systems have no way of identifying or accounting for students in the community college who have reverse-transferred. The literature suggests that researchers are confirming the existence of an increase in undergraduate reverse transfer students (for example, *Counting the Reverse Transfer Student*, 1985; de los Santos and Wright, 1989). Commitment to this research endeavor may reveal even larger numbers of these students on community college campuses.

A number of community college strategic planning and marketing issues are related to the transfer function. The policies that could be affected by the bachelor's degree reverse-transferring function are recruitment and retention, transfer and articulation, and student evaluation of the quality of community college programs and courses. By understanding the needs and characteristics of this reverse transfer market niche, community college leaders can provide numerous training and retraining opportunities, delivered either for credit or noncredit.

## Conclusion

Understanding the special reverse transfer phenomenon is essential to advancing the role, scope, and missions of community colleges. Community colleges have convincingly demonstrated the positive impact that training and education services have had on helping ordinary citizens thrive in local and state economies. It could be that increases in community college enrollments, perhaps attributable to bachelor's degree students enrolling in formal or informal training and education courses, is one of the most phenomenal accessibility stories to embrace the American community colleges. Although more research is needed to prove this point, it is ironic that some bachelor's degree graduates willingly look to the community colleges first for additional training and education.

## References

*Counting the Reverse Transfer Students.* Los Angeles: ERIC Clearinghouse for Junior Colleges, Aug. 1985. (ED 261 757)

de los Santos, A. G., and Wright, I. "Community College and University Student Transfers." *Educational Record,* 1989, 79 (3/4), 82–84.

Missouri Coordinating Board for Higher Education. *1997–1998 Statistical Summary of Missouri Higher Education.* Jefferson City: Department of Higher Education, July 1998.

TERRY L. BARNES *is assistant commissioner of community colleges and technical education for the Missouri Coordinating Board for Higher Education, Jefferson City.*

LAURA M. ROBINSON *is coordinator of institutional surveys and data analysis for Mineral Area College, Park Hills, Missouri, and a doctoral student at the University of Missouri–Columbia.*

*The growing enrollment of baccalaureate degree holders at two-year colleges, as illustrated in studies conducted in Maryland and Tennessee, offers potential institutional problems as well as benefits.*

# Postbaccalaureate Reverse Transfers in Maryland and Tennessee: Institutional Problems and Possibilities

*Barbara K. Townsend, Rivkah Y. Lambert*

Postbaccalaureate reverse transfer students (PRTSs)—two-year college students who already have a baccalaureate degree or higher—present both opportunities and possible problems for the two-year college. Using data from a study of these students in two Maryland community colleges and a study of PRT students in a Tennessee technical institute, we describe (1) why both nondegree and degree-seeking PRTSs attend two-year colleges and what they think of it, (2) what institutional changes or modifications these students would prefer, (3) what institutional problems their presence may create, and (4) how their presence can benefit two-year schools.

During the academic year 1991–92, interviews were conducted with ten randomly selected non-degree-seeking PRTSs from one Maryland community college and ten randomly selected PRTSs pursuing a degree in an allied health program at another Maryland two-year school. Both groups of students were queried about their experiences as community college students and their perceptions of their institutions. Additionally, eight faculty and administrators (four from each college) who were involved with PRTSs (for example, the chair of the allied health program, faculty in the allied program, dean of instruction) were interviewed about the impact of PRTSs on their college and its mission (Lambert, 1994b). A somewhat similar study was conducted in Tennessee in 1997, when all degree-seeking PRTSs at a technical institute (152 students) were surveyed about their reasons for seeking a two-year degree, their evaluation of their two-year experience, and their evaluation of their four-year college experience. Eighty-nine students responded to the survey, and seven of these were subsequently interviewed to explore the survey's questions in more depth. In discussing the Tennessee students, this chapter draws primarily on the interview data.

## Reasons for Attending and Perceptions of the Two-Year College

Whether degree-seeking or non-degree-seeking, most of the PRTSs were attending the two-year school for career-related reasons. Among the Tennessee students surveyed, the most frequently indicated reason was "preparation for career change" (fifty-five respondents, or 62 percent), followed by "personal development" (forty-two respondents, or 48 percent), and "advancement in my current field of employment" (thirty respondents, or 34 percent) (Townsend, 1998). Of the students who were interviewed, only one of the twenty Maryland students and one of the seven Tennessee students were taking courses for personal satisfaction. The Maryland student was learning sign language, and the Tennessee student was majoring in microcomputer technology so he could talk to his two grown sons about computers. Some of the interviewed students were housewives planning to enter the workforce and desiring to learn new skills or update the ones they had learned in their baccalaureate programs. Other students were preparing to change careers or move upward in their current positions. Two students had been laid off and were learning a new field to find employment. As one Tennessee student said, "The two-year degree not only . . . satisfies my necessity of getting back into the job market quickly but it also satisfies the qualifications I will need."

Students in both studies were generally quite satisfied with their educational experiences at the two-year schools. Academically, the institutions provided an excellent fit, not only because of the low costs and convenient course scheduling but because their curricula offered what the students sought: practical, hands-on material that fit their highly focused needs. According to one Tennessee student, "[The college is] up to date with the things that you need to know for my field, which I don't believe the four-year college [I attended] was."

It was the rare student who expressed a desire for more social integration into the two-year college. Most made it clear that they had no time and little desire to attend campus social events. Any time they did have for socializing was spent in preexisting social networks established outside the two-year school. Typical student comments about participating in extracurricular activities included these from two Tennessee students: "I'm not looking for those areas here . . . I just came here to develop my own skills. I wasn't looking for a social venue," and "I couldn't care less . . . I want education and that's it." Only one student in each study expressed the desire to participate in institutional social activities outside the classroom.

All the students in the Tennessee study and almost all the nondegree students in the Maryland study were extremely pleased with two-year college faculty, finding them more approachable and concerned about students than their four-year faculty had been. One Tennessee student said, "The faculty that I've been involved with, 90 percent of them really seem to be concerned with me and how I produce, and they seem to be a little more genuine or something than my experience at [the four-year school I attended as an undergraduate]." Another Tennessee student said, "Here the teachers treat you as an individual. They know you by name and you get more one-on-one help here and there seems to be more tutorial, remedial services here as opposed to a four-year college." A Maryland nondegree student commented, "The instructors are very conscientious, partly because they consider this a mission to make sure we learn correctly what they want to teach us, and they make us work."

An exception to the respect for two-year college teachers was demonstrated by the Maryland students in the allied health program. The program was an extremely selective one, and its content was often taught in baccalaureate programs elsewhere. The curriculum was designed by the American Medical Association (AMA), and completion of the program resulted in the AMA certification necessary to get a job in the field. For several years the majority of students in this program have been PRTSs. This situation may have contributed to what one student perceived as an "intimidating" program in which faculty "treat the students like they are first graders." Another student in the program thought that a couple of his professors were "among the best [he] had ever encountered." At the same time, he had also signed a petition of complaint about one of the instructors. Other students in the program also commented that some of the teachers were great and others were marginal.

## Institutional Modifications Desired by Students

Occasionally, students indicated institutional changes that would facilitate their enrollment and study at the two-year school. Some students felt the colleges needed to construe their possession of a baccalaureate degree as evidence of their ability to perform well academically. Therefore, they should be allowed to take any courses they wanted, even ones for which they had not met the prerequisites. For example, one Maryland nondegree student said, "Even if my degree is twenty years old and I haven't been in the field for ten years, they should allow me to take the course [I want]. If I can't handle it, I'll drop it or I'll walk out of it but give me the opportunity. Don't tell me I have to take one of those stupid AP [Advanced Placement] tests."

Similarly, several Maryland degree-seeking students found it frustrating that they had to undergo the same screening process as all the community college students to determine if they had adequate reading skills for college-level work. When one Maryland degree-seeking student was questioned by college staff to determine whether he had taken English and math, he said, "I had to come down and speak to somebody about it. And I said, 'Look, I've got two associate degrees and I've got a bachelor's degree from the University of Connecticut in the sciences. What do you want to talk about?' And they said, 'Oh, really?' and I said, 'Yes,' and they signed off on [my paper] and that was it."

Although one non-degree-seeking male student thought the college should have "some kind of organization for the older student or the student who already has a degree," most students did not desire counseling, advising about courses, or an orientation session. A typical comment was that of a nondegree-seeking student: "I don't think that older students want to put up with any of the Mickey Mouse junk like counseling they don't think they need. If they have questions, they just want their questions answered." In contrast, another non-degree student said, "I wouldn't mind, but they don't wait until 7:00 at night. I mean, they all leave by what, 4:30, and, you know, they don't make it very convenient to see them." The need for the bookstore and the library to have later hours and weekend hours was also noted.

An institution's financial aid office may need to be more responsive to the needs of some PRTSs. One Tennessee student was frustrated that the college's financial aid office had not provided her with information about special funding she could receive as a laid-off worker. One of her teachers had told her about this aid.

Some of the students in the allied health program were annoyed at the petty bureaucracy. Because one student owed a fifty-cent library fine, he was not allowed to register for the next semester until he went to the bursar's office to pay the fine in person. Another student in the program said of adult students in general, "We just don't have the time to deal with Mickey Mouse standing in line, like to drop this stupid course they told us to drop. First we had to stand in line to register. Then we had to stand in line to drop it. . . . I don't have time to mess around with Mickey Mouse college stuff."

Another example of petty bureaucracy was being asked to submit high school transcripts when the college already had a baccalaureate transcript.

These student complaints suggest that community colleges need to treat PRTSs differently. First of all, some changes should be made in the initial admissions process. The institutional application needs to include a space for students to indicate whether or not they possess a baccalaureate degree or higher so that institutions can maintain better records on the educational backgrounds of their students. Applicants who provide evidence of a baccalaureate degree or higher should be exempted from submitting high school transcripts and taking placement tests in reading and English. A math placement test may still be necessary for certain programs.

Depending on how many PRTSs there are and the college's desire to increase their numbers, student services should be modified to include keeping the bookstore, library, and counseling services open during at least some evenings and weekends. Other student services might include recreational opportunities targeted at this student group. Also, any services that could be conducted on-line such as course enrollments and withdrawals or paying of fees would benefit not only PRTSs but all community college students.

## Possible Institutional Problems in Enrolling PRTSs

The presence of PRTSs may be a challenge for some faculty, requiring accommodations on their part. Enrollment of these students also raises questions regarding institutional mission.

PRTSs may be more prone than first-time, undergraduate, two-year students to question and challenge faculty, even question them about grades and course content. For example, one Maryland degree-seeking student described what happened when she received a grade she didn't agree with: "I looked over things, got a whole arsenal of books, tromped up there with my arsenal and said, 'Look at this and this and this and this,' and I got my grade changed. . . . I guess there is an advantage to having gone through college before." Another Maryland student told how she behaved when she thought faculty were "giving blatantly wrong information. I've gone up to them after class alone not to embarrass anyone and I usually bring some supportive evidence. And they'll say, 'Yup, you're right.'"

PRTSs particularly resent any approaches they view as demeaning to their adult status. For example, a couple of Maryland degree-seeking students complained about "the kindergarten approach to learning" in their program. One student said, "Someone will come along and grade your work with a little red pencil. That gets old." Another student complained that when an instructor gave a test, he told students to move their desks apart, every other chair. The student's reaction to this request was, "I'm like, am I in grade school, you know? Am I in first grade? Like I'm really going to cheat off the person next to me. I mean, I'm in college. I don't need to be spoken to this way."

There is also the risk of faculty teaching to these students at the expense of other students. One division chair observed that PRTSs are students who "will ask a real [sic] stimulating question and you might want to go off on a tangent and answer their question, and you'll look around and see that you've lost 90 percent of the class . . . and then you realize that you've got to come back." This same person said that PRTSs can also be "perfectly obnoxious. They can try to monopolize the class and in a very structured curriculum like nursing, the other students will actually dislike them."

Beyond the level of possible problems in the classroom, Templin (1983) has queried whether admitting PRTSs is antithetical to the mission of the two-year college. From his perspective, the institution is a second chance for those who did not do well in K–12 education. For PRTSs, it becomes an opportunity for a second chance in the job market, as John and Melissa Quinley indicate in Chapter Four. From a policy perspective the concern is that PRTSs potentially receive their second chance at the expense of other students, especially those for whom the two-year college was designed. An analogous situation may be the enrollment of white students at historically black colleges. When this happens, some "blacks fear the loss of an institution that represents their cultural heritage . . . black students feel that they are being pushed out and thereby deprived of an education" (Elam, quoted in Hazard, 1988, pp. 17–18).

When asked how they viewed the enrollment of PRTSs in relation to the two-year college's mission, the Maryland administrators had differing opinions. Some saw no conflict with mission; others did. Typical of the no-conflict position is the following comment about the fact that most students in the competitive allied health program already have baccalaureate degrees: "I don't have any problem with it at all. I think if we're serving the community, we are serving the needs of the state, and the state includes people with bachelor's degrees who do not have an opportunity to take [this] training elsewhere." Similarly, a Maryland faculty member had this to say about these students: "The college is providing a service in training individuals who could go out and serve this area. . . . It's sort of like, you can look at it as continuing education."

Other administrators and faculty were more ambivalent. One said:

> A part of me says that this is a community college to serve the needs of the community, and if you come and you're a part of the community and you've got a need and you fit the criteria, well more power to you. Then there's the other side of me that knows that, in all of our [allied health] programs, we have a limited number of students we take, and . . . these students are beating out the others for these spots, and it isn't fair. . . . I think that we as a college would not be following our mission exactly if we continue to cater to the postbaccalaureate students. They make teaching very wonderful and very worthwhile, but they're not the only students.

Similarly, an associate dean of instruction was concerned about the effect of considering receipt of the baccalaureate degree in determining admissions to the highly selective physician assistant program.

> We would not stop serving those students because they're a part of the mix and the diversity that we're here to address. But we have to be careful about the exclusivity that can result from making their previous educational experience a really important factor for admission at the expense of other people who could benefit from that educational experience and who could be successful eventually . . . we need to continue to strive to meet the needs of [PRTSs]. . . . I don't have a problem with that as long as it is part of our effort to meet the varied needs of the varied constituencies, not to the exclusion of other parts of the population that we have an equal obligation to.

A division chair offered a number of practical solutions to the problem of admitting PRTSs at the expense of people new to college. One solution is to admit degree-seeking students before admitting certificate-seeking students. That way, the PRTSs who want a certificate would not be admitted before students who seek a two-year degree. Another solution is to teach some of the courses PRTSs take as noncredit courses, for example, "teach AutoCAD noncredit." Also, "if there has to be a pecking order, the people who are already employed in a field related to a discipline would have to take noncredit until a seat opened up." Another possibility is to open up more seats by hiring more instructors in selective programs. Although not suggested by any of those interviewed, another solution would be to have PRTSs pay more for their courses. This approach was tried briefly in California in the early 1990s, and enrollment of PRTSs dropped precipitously (Trombley, 1993).

## Institutional Benefits of Enrolling PRTSs

Although problematic at times, enrolling PRTSs can also be beneficial to a two-year college. These students can assist fellow students, positively affect class-room dynamics, demonstrate appropriate student behavior, stimulate and challenge the faculty academically, and serve as good public relations for the college.

PRTSs can provide informal tutoring and academic advising to fellow students. Almost all the Maryland students who were seeking a degree in an allied health field spoke about forming study groups and tutoring each other. A Maryland non-degree student said, "I do a little bit of helping out when I can. People will ask me, 'Did you get this?'" One of the Tennessee students told how she encouraged some of her fellow students to go to a four-year school after attending the two-year school.

> I would say you need to move on, I mean you have such a talent, this would be so good for you to keep fostering this creativity or fostering this talent that you have. And they would say, oh, I don't have any money. . . . And I'd say, well, there's books . . . books that tell you where to research for scholarship money.

A non-degree-seeking female taking an introductory computer course said she turned to fellow students for help. In her late thirties, she stated that "the younger students were just more adept. They knew a lot more what to do on the computer than [my computer lab partner and I] did. If I had a little problem, they were the ones to say, OK, this is what you're supposed to do."

PRTSs in the classroom can influence class dynamics positively. For example, one Maryland non-degree-seeking female said:

> As one of the better students in the classroom, I think I'm picking out . . . a lot of dynamic about what's going on with the other students. Somebody will ask a question and it's clear they don't know what they're talking about. Sometimes the question won't be addressed by the instructor. Either they [the instructors] don't understand the question or they got off on part of it or whatever. And I will focus the class on what I perceive the problem to actually be. I raise my hand and clarify the question . . . restate the question and focus the instructor on what he missed and what this person is missing. I try not to let the class drift away. I sort of feel a responsibility to . . . the whole group to keep people focused.

Similarly, another Maryland non-degree-seeking student commented, "I'm the one who sits in the front and asks a zillion questions. Not everyone's like that."

According to the Maryland faculty and administrators who were interviewed, PRTSs are knowledgeable about how to operate in an academic setting and demonstrate this knowledge in the classroom. One division chair said, "They know that in class they're supposed to ask questions and to respond to questions. . . . They'd also know how to write a paper and they'd know something real simple like that a paper has a beginning, a middle, and an end. And someone with a baccalaureate degree will know how to use the system. They'll know how to go to the library and get help. They'll know who to go to on campus."

One person reflected that in the human development class that he taught, "people who have degrees stick right out in that course . . . they have some comfort with batting around intellectual ideas." Also, the PRTSs students "were just intellectually much more comfortable with reading, answering questions, writing papers, whatever. And they wanted additional readings." A division chair described these students as "generally bring[ing] much more thought-provoking questions and much more significant issues to the table, particularly if they've had broad experiences. They'll read between the lines in the textbook that some students may not bring to the class and consequently liven the discussion and make it [a] much more thorough presentation of the discipline."

Believing that PRTSs are "better students, and better students in the classroom help students that are not the better students," one division chair even suggested that knowledge of how to teach PRTSs be incorporated into a faculty development effort. He suggested it be titled "Enhancing Instruction by Using Baccalaureate-Holding Students in the Classroom." An associate dean of instruction suggested using PRTSs "as an educational resource for other students." He advocated developing "some kind of mentoring relationship between the student who has had that kind of educational experience and students who are new and young and right out of high school."

PRTSs can also challenge and stimulate the faculty academically. As one faculty member said:

> You get a lot more esoteric questions. They need the bigger picture. . . . So you have to be prepared to give them what they need or guide them in the direction of where they can get it. . . . You have to be more on your toes. They don't accept answers like, "Well, that's not within the scope of this course." You know, all those standard things that instructors use when they don't know the answer to a question. You just have to say, "I'm not familiar with that. That's not been my experience." I'll check it out and give them resources. And basically, it's like a willingness to listen to them and acknowledge their skill level.

Similarly, an administrator said, "They'll come up after class and they'll talk more and ask questions. They're more probing."

PRTSs can also be a source of excellent public relations for the college. Prior to attending the institution, as taxpayers they were usually supporting the institution as one more government-sponsored entity. After attending the college, they know first-hand the benefits it provides the community. One administrator suggested they be "use[d] in testimonials, where they could say, 'I've spent five years in college: four at a university and one at a community college. And the greatest year was in the community college.'"

## Conclusion

In discussing the motivation of postbaccalaureate reverse transfers, one Maryland administrator said:

> They're very motivated and very interested, sometimes for reasons that are rather sad. They've gotten their [four-year] degree but they did not find a position or the position is not what they envisioned it to be and now they're coming back. They're gonna 'start all over.' [As a result,] they're more focused, they're more disciplined, they're more mature, they're more interested [than the eighteen-year-old community college student].

This comment poignantly describes why many PRTSs go to the two-year college. They need a second chance in the job market, some because they "have been harmed by the economic system in a different way than the truly disadvantaged" and some because they realize they've chosen the wrong career and want preparation for one more personally meaningful. Additionally, longer life spans and changing gender roles contribute to some older women seeking new job skills or brushing up rusty ones so they can reenter the job market after having stayed out to raise a family.

Responding to these students' educational needs creates a dilemma for faculty and administrators who are concerned about the two-year college's social service role. A second chance for PRTSs may come at the expense of a second chance for a major group of students served by the contemporary, public, two-year college: those people who did not do well in K–12 education and can only get jobs requiring a high school diploma or less. Without some postsecondary education, they will be unable to "move from the bottom levels of the labor force into mid-skilled positions" (Grubb, 1996, p. 87). As Lambert (1994a) notes, "Those community colleges whose cachement area includes many college-educated residents and/or whose curricula include a large number of allied health and other technology-based occupational programs . . . are the most likely to confront the philosophical and theoretical issues that arise from . . . enrollment [of PRTSs]" (p. 61).

Depending on a particular community's demographics and economic situation, some two-year schools could potentially emerge as the site of low-cost retooling for the academically capable and credentialed middle-class. Although enrolling PRTSs is appropriate, given the community college's mission of providing lifelong learning, institutional leaders need to ensure that these students' enrollment does not displace the economically and academically disadvantaged individuals for whom the community college may be the only chance to gain postsecondary education.

## References

Grubb, N. *Working in the Middle: Strengthening Education and Training for the Mid-Skilled Labor Force.* San Francisco: Jossey-Bass, 1996.

Hazard, T. *Attitudes and Perceptions of White Students Attending Historically Black Colleges and Universities.* Unpublished report. Tallahassee, Fla.: Department of Education Leadership, June 1988.

Lambert, R. Y. "College Graduates in Maryland's Community Colleges." *The MAHE Journal,* 1994a, *17,* 61–69.

Lambert, R. Y. "College-Wise: Post-Baccalaureate Reverse Transfer Students Attending Baltimore Community Colleges." Unpublished doctoral dissertation, University of Maryland, 1994b.

Templin, R. "Keeping the Door Open for Disadvantaged Students." In G. Vaughan (ed.), *Issues for Community College Leaders in a New Era.* San Francisco: Jossey-Bass, 1983.

Townsend, B. K. "Reverse Diploma Transfer Students in a Technical Institute." Paper presented at the annual meeting of the American Educational Research Association, San Diego, Apr. 1998.

Trombley, W. *Public Policy by Anecdote: The Case of Community College Fees.* San Jose: California Higher Education Policy Center, 1993.

BARBARA K. TOWNSEND *is professor of higher education at the University of Missouri–Columbia. While a professor at the University of Memphis, she worked in the Office of Academic Affairs on transfer and articulation issues. She is a former community college faculty member and administrator.*

RIVKAH Y. LAMBERT *is assistant to the deans for outreach programs at Baltimore Hebrew University.*

*The operational and public policy challenges associated with increasing numbers of reverse transfer students are examined.*

# Institutional and Public Policy Implications of the Phenomenon of Reverse Transfer Students

*Daniel J. Phelan*

Community colleges were established in the dawn of the twentieth century to fulfill several needs in our society. Although several purposes were developed for these colleges, their charter included the tantamount responsibility of being open-door, open-access institutions. Over the years, these institutions witnessed phenomenal growth and expansion due to their success in meeting the needs of their constituency. Success led to success as the function and number of colleges grew to meet burgeoning federal, state, and local needs. Now, nearly a century later, the continuation of the open-door mission may be in danger. This risk is due, in large measure, to declining federal and state assistance, increasing levels of accountability required by its various publics, and an increasing demand for additional programs and services.

A specific and rising contributor to the limiting of the open-door mission, particularly in large metropolitan areas, is the growing enrollment of the reverse transfer student. In fact, for some institutions, reverse transfer student enrollments have displaced other students without an associate degree, diploma, or certificate. Consequently, students, parents, administrators, boards, and policymakers are now questioning the appropriateness of this community college function.

Although postsecondary education leading to transfer to a baccalaureate-granting institution has always been a core mission of the community college, reverse transfer activity is a relatively new phenomenon. Data concerning the actual volume of reverse transfer students on a state-by-state basis are largely unknown. Currently, databases maintained at federal and state levels are not structured to track this type of information.

Given that community colleges across the nation enrolled 5.5 million students in the 1998 fall semester (American Association of Community Colleges, 1998), the potential numbers of reverse transfer students could be substantial. Even a conservative estimate of 15 to 20 percent of the nation's community college enrollment represents 825,000 to 1.1 million students. This estimated volume of reverse transfer student activity will have a considerable impact on institutional, state, and federal budgets, as well as general institutional operations.

Increasing numbers of reverse transfer students enrolling in the community college may be seen, by some institutions, as a boon, while others see these students putting added stresses on an infrastructure pushed to the limit. The specific challenges posed by reverse transfer students suggest a number of institutional and public policy issues that must be considered. In this chapter I explore eight of the more significant implications of reverse transfer students for higher education institutional operations, college and university administration, state and federal government, and for students themselves. The listing, while not exhaustive, is designed to promote dialogue and encourage the development of a thoughtful policysetting approach and response to the needs of reverse transfer students. Absent the creation of such a planned approach and general philosophy, any actions taken could result in negative outcomes, not only for the student but for the institution and state as well.

## Limited State Legislative Support

Competition for state dollars continues to rise, even among higher education institutions within a state. Although state legislators bear the responsibility to provide basic support for a coordinated and comprehensive system of higher education, they also seek the means to reduce the budget and reduce taxes. As Soche (1994) observed, "States simply have too many fiscal obligations, too many special interests competing for scarce resources, and too many debts to heed higher education's urgent pleas for more money. . . . States have to reserve larger and larger chunks of their budgets for such things as Medicaid and prisons, for which the courts or laws require certain spending levels. That leaves higher education and other 'discretionary' services to fight for an increasingly smaller plate of scraps" (p. 71).

State legislators still have not forged the relationship between economic development and continuous education of the populace. Rather, legislators find themselves needing to stem the rise of state aid to higher education. For policymakers, providing additional assistance to postbaccalaureate reverse transfers at community colleges seems to be fiscally redundant.

Given the fiscal limitations of state legislatures and the community college's mission to respond to student needs, its board members may be left to increase tuition as another means of generating revenues necessary to operate a college. Consequently, community college students face increasingly higher tuition bills. The threat of limited state funding, combined with pricing tuition out of reach for many students, may not permit the existence of a reverse transfer pathway.

## Enrollment Implications for Four-Year Institutions

As studies discussed in Chapter One indicated, many reverse transfers seem to find the traditional four-year model of higher education outmoded and no longer adequate for their specific needs. Both undergraduate reverse transfers and postbaccalaureate students are attracted to the community college because of its relatively low cost, its ability to provide timely and marketable education for the life-long learner, and its perceived educational relevance to the needs of employers.

It is this last strength—the ability to prepare students to meet employers' needs—that is so valued by policymakers. A recent survey, conducted by the Midwestern Higher Education Commission (MHEC), polled multistate political leaders to ascertain their priorities for higher education. Results indicate that lawmakers needed the higher education industry to improve on its ability to meet the requirements of the employing community (1998). However, in the same report, political leaders ranked "insuring affordability," "establishing accountability," and "productivity and cost efficiency," higher than being responsive to employer needs. Policymakers, particularly at four-year colleges, may find that these particular issues are at cross purposes.

Finally, baccalaureate-granting colleges and universities, in order to discourage the loss of enrollments, may need to consider some program and course modifications as well as new recruitment strategies. In addition, these institutions may find it proactive, even desirable, to work directly with community colleges to combine efforts and meet the needs of the reverse transfer student.

## Defining the Reverse Transfer Rate and State Priority

As stated previously, a complete and clear understanding of the nature, behaviors, and motivations of reverse transfer students is lacking in most states. Before institutional and state policies become calcified, it is incumbent on higher education leaders to further define reverse transfer and the rate of activity. Furthermore, dialogue with lawmakers needs to fully consider reverse transfer in terms of state priorities such as economic development and global competitiveness.

Slark (1982, p. 4) cites a number of questions asked by both legislators and higher education personnel regarding the reverse transfer student:

> Are these students returning to the community college because they experienced academic difficulty at the four-year college?; Was the four-year college too costly?; Is there a particular major(s) or school(s) which is more often returning students?; Are reverse transfers returning with BA degrees to learn a trade?; Or are they largely students engaging in lifelong learning and self-growth pursuits?

Until such time as these questions and others like them can be adequately answered, reverse transfer students will not be understood or supported as they relate to a state's higher education priorities. Worse yet, undesirable policies could be established that could be punitive to students and community colleges because of poor or incomplete information.

## Metropolitan Versus Rural Institutions

Although the enrollment of reverse transfer students is becoming substantial, the relative effect on community colleges will depend on the geographical location, and hence the current enrollment levels, of any particular community college. The majority of the nation's nearly twelve hundred community colleges are located in rural areas. As such, these institutions tend to have excess enrollment capacity capable of absorbing reverse transfer students. Conversely, many metropolitan and urban community colleges, by virtue of their location, tend to be at enrollment capacity. Consequently, the marginal cost of adding a transfer student at a rural community college is likely to be significantly smaller in comparison to that of metro or urban community colleges. Unfortunately, as observed by Callan (1997), "Governors and legislators, particularly those in our most populous states, sometimes inappropriately treat all community colleges in their states as if they were virtually identical. They find the task of tailoring laws to meet the needs of the many different members of so diverse a group to be beyond easy solution" (p. 96). Policymakers, in considering the increasing volume of reverse transfer students, will need to evaluate this disparity between institutions in order to arrive at an appropriate solution.

## Impact on the Mission of the Community Colleges

As previously stated, community colleges have existed for decades as open-door institutions. However, when faced with limited funding and burgeoning enrollments, the question becomes, For whom should the community college provide services? As indicated in previous chapters, the community college may now find itself in a potential mission dilemma. One option for dealing with this barrier is to eliminate the "comprehensive" mission that has defined the community college movement since its beginning. These two-year institutions could become "niche community colleges" (Phelan, 1997), providing only a portion of the services they have in the past and focusing instead on institutional strengths and regional demands.

The requirements placed on community colleges continue to increase and have, in some cases, outstripped their ability to meet those demands. Consequently, a number of community colleges have, since the early 1990s, engaged in the use of enrollment caps. These admissions maximums, by virtue of their existence, prompt the sorting of students.

In California, for example, the state's community college enrollments alone are projected to increase by over 18 percent during the next eight years, nearly 348,000 students. As a result, California sought in the early 1990s to incorporate the prioritization of students who wish to use the community college by limiting state subsidies to community colleges for current degree holders.

In 1993 legislators levied "a $50-per-unit 'differential fee'" (Trombley, 1993, p. 1) for baccalaureate holders wanting to take community college courses. The result was a decline in enrollments so drastic that the fee was later phased out (Gose, 1997).

California's earlier experience with enrollment reduction strategies has not fared well with the public. The institutions' constituents continue to articulate the need for equal access to higher education (Callan, 1997). The preferential enrollment priority given first-time students in that state seems a difficult challenge at best. The principal policy concerns continue to focus on limiting student opportunities through restrictive access measures.

In contrast, if no method for sorting students is established, and all students are allowed to compete equally, reverse transfer students are likely, by virtue of their skills obtained from previous education, to edge out first-time students. Furthermore, community college instructional programs with selective admissions requirements, typically allied health and related programs, may place an even greater restriction on first-time students. It would seem that some modification to current enrollment methods might be indicated in order to serve both student groups.

From a policy standpoint, lawmakers may need to reconsider the comprehensive mission of their state's community colleges. Should the economically and academically disadvantaged of the community college constituency receive top enrollment priority? Perhaps community colleges, due to fiscal constraints, will need to reconsider being "all things to all people" and focus on identified institutional strengths and the needs specific to their region. In some communities, though, that may be serving reverse transfer students.

## Economic Development Implications

The business and industrial community understands that, in order to remain globally competitive, worker training, retraining, and capacity building are essential on an ongoing basis. "Nearly 100 percent of this nation's employers indicate that all their existing workers will need additional training by the year 2000" (Zeiss, 1998, p. 11). Many of the workers needing training will be reverse transfer students, possessing not only baccalaureate degrees but also master's and doctoral degrees.

These students, as well as businesses and industries, acknowledge community colleges as a solution to their training needs. However, this preferred position is at risk. As Zeiss (1998, p. 11) states:

> Community colleges may lose their best opportunity in history to become the economic engines of our country and meet the latest needs of our communities, unless those who regulate and operate colleges can effect changes soon. Essentially, we must reduce bureaucracy in our colleges by convincing policymakers, regulators, and faculty and staff that market sensitivity is a core value along with quality instruction and student learning. Providing market-based learning must become a cornerstone of our community-based mission.

Precluding the enrollment of reverse transfer students will run counter to a long-standing economic development mission of the community colleges.

## Implications for Financial Aid

A primary policy question involving reverse transfer students involves their access to federal financial aid through the Higher Education Act, Title IV Aid. The cost of community college attendance is composed of direct costs and indirect costs. Traditional limitations do apply, however, including semester credit hours enrolled, degree status, and borrowing amounts. Additionally, financial aid cannot be spread among multiple institutions attended by a single student.

Although a student must be considered "degree seeking" to obtain a student loan, the degree being sought need not be in the traditional progression of associate degree first, bachelor's degree second, master's third, and so forth. Consequently, no restriction for reverse transfer students exists as long as they remain degree seeking. Additionally, campus work study funds are neither dependent on degree-seeking status nor degree progression. However, reverse transfer students may be precluded from accessing Pell Grants or Supplemental Education Opportunity Grants (SEOG) and similar types of aid, depending on degree status. Specifically, undergraduate reverse transfers would be eligible to access Pell funds; however, postbaccalaureate reverse transfer students would not. Current federal language considers the attainment of a bachelor's degree as a culminating award. Essentially, as long as students do not complete the bachelor's degree, they are eligible for grant aid.

Policymakers will need to consider the implications of financial assistance for reverse transfer students. In the case of grant aid (PELL and SEOG), federal provisions for accessing these funds may discourage students from advancing to the culminating award. Placing additional restrictions on financial aid access will most certainly impede reverse transfer behaviors.

## Market Demand and Taxpayer Rights

Given the practical marketplace realities of lifelong learning, retraining, and technological advancement prompted by increasing global competition, community colleges have continued to respond to their environment. Reverse transfer students represent the latest entrée into the ever-increasing lineup of community needs. With community college operations largely tax supported or tax assisted by local constituencies, remaining accessible to the public is vital for political, financial, and economic reasons.

A more recent congressional enactment, The Taxpayer Relief Act of 1997 (Public Law 105-34), added section 25A to the Internal Revenue Code to provide the Lifetime Learning Credit, that is, education credits. This program essentially encourages persons to continue their education, which could include reverse transfer education taken at a community college. In general, the Lifetime Learning Credit allows student taxpayers to claim a nonrefundable credit against their federal income taxes for certain postsecondary educational expenses, although an education credit in excess of a taxpayer's tax liability cannot be refunded.

The policy implications of market and taxpayer demands on the community college suggest that accessibility should be maintained for reverse transfer students. Concomitantly, there should be no penalization of instructional quality.

## Conclusion

As community colleges have grown in size and mission over the years, increasing constituency demands were often managed by adding class sections, building new campuses, increasing tuition, adding additional staff, and opening new programs. Reverse transfer students at community colleges may not be so easily managed, however.

The complexities of community college involvement with reverse transfer students do not allow for simple solutions. At the very heart of the issue is the unique role that community colleges have played as open-door institutions, providing access to all students who possessed the ability to benefit. Indeed, the community college role and mission now come into question, not only from an institutional perspective but from state and federal public policy points of view. Declining federal and state resources in the face of increasing enrollments and constituent demands further exacerbate this discussion.

At an even more basic level is the fundamental question of whether education for reverse transfer students, provided by community colleges, should be considered a public good or a private good. Should the taxpaying community encourage enrollment of these students, or should this cost be borne by the business and industry community?

The references to "comprehensive community college" and "open-door college" have aptly described the mission of the community college in this country. However, these institutions face ever-increasing demands of their constituency, while concurrently dealing with declining resources. A common approach to evaluating policy implications of reverse transfer students could help to redefine enrollment practices and potentially augment declining college resources. Nevertheless, legislators may also need to consider whether the open-door mission is still sustainable.

This chapter has reviewed some of the principal policy implications of the reverse transfer student for institutions, as well as state and federal higher education leaders. Although not exhaustive, these issues are intended to evoke discussion, the gathering of data, and the development of a coherent policy for the handling and management of reverse transfer students at the community college level.

## References

American Association of Community Colleges. "American Association of Community Colleges 1998 Facts." Brochure. Washington, D.C.: American Association of Community Colleges, 1998.

Callan, P. M. "Stewards of Opportunity: America's Public Community Colleges." *Daedalus,* 1997, *126* (4), 95–112.

Gose, B. "A Community College in Virginia Attracts Ph.D.'s—as Students. *Chronicle of Higher Education,* July 11, 1997, pp. A33–34.

Midwestern Higher Education Commission. "Higher Education Policy Issues in the Midwestern States: Results from a Survey of State Political Leaders and Higher Education Leaders." Minneapolis: Midwestern Higher Education Commission, 1998.

Phelan, D. J. "The Niche Community College: Is It Our Future?" *Community College Journal,* 1997, *67* (4), 30–33.

Slark, J. "Reverse Transfer Student Study." Santa Ana, Calif.: Santa Ana College, 1982. (ED 221 248)

Soche, G. *The Fall of the Ivory Tower: Government Funding, Corruption, and the Bankrupting of American Higher Education.* Washington, D.C.: Regnery, 1994.

Trombley, W. H. *Public Policy by Anecdote: The Case of Community College Fees.* San Jose: California Higher Education Policy Center, Apr. 1993.

Zeiss, T. "The Realities of Competition: Will Our Students Become Theirs?" *Community College Journal,* 1998, *68* (6), 8–13.

DANIEL J. PHELAN *is president of Southeastern Community College, Merged Area XVI, West Burlington and Keokuk, Iowa.*

*A review of recent ERIC literature demonstrates researchers' attempts to define reverse transfer students, describe their complex enrollment patterns, and understand the implications for institutions.*

# Sources and Information on the Scope and Impact of Reverse Transfers

*Christine M. LeBard*

In the educational pipeline, community colleges have long been considered an intermediate step in the vertical progression of students from high school to four-year colleges and universities. According to this traditional perspective, two-year colleges serve a transfer function by allowing students to earn credits, certificates, or associate degrees prior to enrolling in four-year institutions, where they presumably will earn a baccalaureate degree. Individuals who follow this standard transfer pattern still represent a significant proportion of the student movement between two-year and four-year institutions. However, a growing number are students following more complex enrollment patterns. These students often have attended four-year institutions prior to enrolling in community college—a behavior antithetical to the traditional pipeline model. The emergence of these variations has complicated the tasks of researchers, administrators, and policymakers, who struggle to gauge the scope and implications of this growing phenomenon.

A review of documents submitted to the ERIC database over the past decade demonstrates the complexity of issues arising from this diversification of the transfer student population. This chapter enumerates some of the primary concerns: defining the population, understanding its demographics, tracking student progress, responding to unique needs, and planning for the future.

## Difficulty of Tracking Reverse Transfers

The difficulty in finding recent literature on this growing phenomenon of students attending community college after enrolling in four-year institutions indicates the difficulty that researchers encounter in tracking these students.

Perhaps the problem stems from the variety of terms that have been used to identify students who follow these nontraditional transfer patterns. *Reverse transfer students* or *returning transfer students* are two of the most common designations. In addition to searching the ERIC database with these keywords, additional resources can be located by combining search terms such as *transfer* with *baccalaureate degree holders*. Linking these two categories captures the literature pertaining to students who returned to the two-year college after earning the baccalaureate. As indicated in previous chapters, these students often are considered to be *postbaccalaureate reverse transfer students*.

Typically, reverse transfer students are those who began higher education at four-year institutions and then transferred to two-year colleges before attaining the baccalaureate. The literature reveals, however, that this label is often altered to fit the specific purpose of a study. For example, the Contra Costa Community College District (CCCCD) in California conducted a districtwide study to determine the type and number of transfer students served by the district, as well as the University of California, the California State University, and St. Mary's College between 1982–83 and 1989–90 (Baratta, 1992). This study employed the term *new reverse-transfer students* and defined this group as "students who enrolled in a CCCCD college for the first time after attending a four-year institution" (p. 4).

In their eighth-year report of the New Start Program at Kingsborough Community College (part of the City University of New York), Winchell and Schwartz do not refer to program participants as reverse transfers (1993). Nevertheless, these students do fit the generally accepted definition because "New Start is a program for students who began their higher education at certain senior colleges but did not do well there" (p. 3). This not only describes the enrollment behavior of reverse transfer students but it illuminates their rationale for transferring to the community college.

These two examples demonstrate that administrators and researchers do not necessarily use the same language to define and describe similar segments of their student population. Such variation contributes to the difficulty in understanding the reverse transfer phenomenon on a national, statewide, or even local level.

Adding to the complexity is the further distinction between reverse transfer students and returning transfer students. For example, the CCCCD study defined *returning transfer students* as "students who previously were enrolled in a CCCCD college, transferred to a four-year system, left, and re-enrolled in a CCCCD college" (1992, p. 3). There is general agreement among authors of documents in the ERIC database that students engaging in this enrollment pattern—two-year college, four-year institution, two-year college—are considered returning transfer students.

Understanding the concept of reverse transfer becomes more complex as researchers distinguish between prebaccalaureate and postbaccalaureate students. Chan and McIntyre (1995) identify baccalaureate degree holders as "completer reverse transfers" and define them as "those who transferred from a four-year institution after earning a bachelor's degree or higher" (p. 4).

In Trombley's (1993) report, "Public Policy by Anecdote," he recounts some of the legislative discussions leading up to the implementation of differential fees in California for community college students with bachelor's degrees. Supporters of this bill made frequent references to "rich housewives" (p. 4), implying that postbaccalaureate reverse transfers were enrolling in community college for personal enrichment reasons and therefore siphoning off scarce resources. In the aftermath of the fee increase, enrollment plummeted. This demonstrates that workforce training and skills upgrading, rather than developing personal interests, are more common reasons for baccalaureate degree holders to attend community college.

The examples indicate that degree status (prebaccalaureate or postbaccalaureate) and original institution of enrollment (two-year or four-year) are the most common criteria for classifying students within the broad category of reverse transfer. However, as the New Start program and California's differential fee experiment indicate, it also is critical to examine students' reasons for transferring to community colleges, at both the prebaccalaureate and postbaccalaureate stages.

Having recognized the dilemmas associated with defining and describing the students who follow nontraditional transfer patterns, the remaining sections of this chapter address issues affecting these students as a whole. The general term *reverse transfer student* will be used.

## Reverse Transfer Rates

Institutions' keen interest in tracking the numbers of reverse transfer students and following their academic progress is reflected in the ERIC literature. For example, Bers (1992) examined transfer patterns of Oakton College (Illinois) students by using a dataset of all students who received a bachelor's degree from an Illinois public university between 1980 and 1988. Of the 6,074 students in the dataset for whom Oakton attendance could be verified, 28 percent (1,678) had attended after receiving their bachelor's degrees. Of these postbaccalaureate reverse transfer students, 612 also attended Oakton before receiving their bachelor's degrees.

In California, Chan and McIntyre (1995) found that 38,400 students transferred from the University of California and California State University systems to two-year colleges in 1983. Baratta (1992) reported that 12.9 percent of the students served by the Contra Costa Community College District were reverse transfers and 10.8 percent were returning transfer students. Trombley's report (1993) highlights the impact of reverse transfer students at California's community colleges by emphasizing that sixty thousand (48 percent) of the students who held baccalaureate degrees dropped out due to the differential fee effect of the early 1990s. He also reports that three out of five baccalaureate-degree-holding students return to two-year colleges for job training or upgrading of skills.

A comprehensive examination of the reverse transfer phenomenon at the national level is lacking. However, McCormick and Carroll's (1997) preliminary analysis indicates that about half of the nation's students who transferred from four-year institutions can be categorized as reverse transfers.

The growing complexity of student enrollment patterns is not unique to the United States. Vaala (1991) described an on-going investigation of student mobility from four-year to two-year colleges in Alberta, Canada. Nearly 20 percent of the students in the sample had attended another postsecondary institution before enrolling at their current two-year college. Generally, the students who had transferred from universities were studying a different content area at the two-year college.

## Demographics of Reverse Transfer Students

In addition to illustrating the difficulties involved with defining and tracking reverse transfer students, literature in the ERIC database also provides demographic data for this population. Ethnicity, gender, age, and degree attainment are some common variables examined.

**Ethnicity.**  Kinnick and others (1997) studied the student flow patterns among three community colleges and Portland State University in Oregon by using a random sample of 504 students. They found that more than half of the reverse transfer students in their sample were Asian American. These Asian American students also were more likely to move among various institutions than were other minority students. African American students, however, displayed more traditional enrollment patterns. Fifty-three percent of African Americans moved directly from two-year college to four-year institutions, compared to 33 percent of other minority students, and 47 percent of white students (Kinnick and others, 1997).

The Oklahoma State Regents for Higher Education (1997) compiled a student transfer matrix that reported the numbers of students transferring among higher education institutions within the state. Data were provided by receiving institutions. The report indicated that 1,089 students transferred from Oklahoma State University to other public institutions. Of this group, 26 percent transferred to two-year institutions. Examination of this sample by ethnic group showed that Asian Americans and whites had the highest reverse-transfer rates (27 percent for both).

Unlike the two state-specific studies, McCormick and Carroll's (1997) examination of the spring 1994 follow-up data to the 1990 Beginning Postsecondary Students Longitudinal Study determined that Asian and Pacific Islanders were least likely to transfer from four-year to two-year institutions. Their reverse transfer rate was 14 percent, compared to 29 to 31 percent for other ethnic groups for whom a transfer rate could be estimated.

**Gender.**  Vaala's (1991) study of students at a two-year college in Alberta, Canada, found that more males than females had previously attended a university. In Kajstura and Keim's (1992) study of 525 reverse transfer students in Illinois, women (56 percent) outnumbered men.

Both Kinnick and others' (1997) study of students in Oregon and McCormick and Carroll's (1997) examination of a national data set report no significant differences between men and women with regard to reverse transfer behavior. Although McCormick and Carroll (1997) report that men were more likely to experience nontraditional enrollment patterns, the difference was not significant.

**Age.** These two studies also found that students over the age of twenty were more likely to engage in multiple transfers between institutions, including transfer from four-year to two-year colleges. Kinnick and others (1997) divided their sample into several age categories to determine correlations between age and transfer patterns. Fifty-two percent of students between sixteen and twenty-one in their study transferred once, 23 percent transferred twice, and 26 percent transferred three or more times. Students between the ages of twenty-two and thirty tended to move more frequently. Forty-two percent of this group transferred once, 21 percent transferred twice, and 36 percent transferred three or more times. Students over the age of thirty-one appeared to move least, with 63 percent transferring only once. McCormick and Carroll (1997) analyzed just two groups, those under twenty and those twenty and older. They determined that older students were more likely to follow nontraditional enrollment patterns.

## Reasons for Reverse Transfer

Receiving occupational training, upgrading skills, and pursuing personal interests are common reasons for students to enroll in community colleges after attending four-year institutions. By examining the transfer behavior among students who began their postsecondary education in 1989–90, McCormick and Carroll (1997) determined that 22 percent of the prebaccalaureates who reverse transferred had completed a bachelor's degree by 1994 or were reenrolled at a four-year institution. In addition, McCormick and Carroll found that students whose highest aspirations were to attain the bachelor's degree were more likely to experience reverse transfer than those who sought to attain more advanced degrees.

Among Illinois reverse transfer students, the five most important reasons students gave for leaving their four-year institutions before earning the baccalaureate degree were personal reasons, financial reasons, academic difficulty, career change, and inability to decide on academic or career goals (Kajstura and Keim, 1992). Their reasons for enrolling in a two-year college were proximity to home, low tuition, convenient class times, instructional quality, job training opportunity, GPA improvement, and relatives' or friends' advice.

Baccalaureate degree holders were likewise served in Oregon through community colleges. Of the 382 students who entered the University of Portland State (UPS) through community colleges, 8 percent were postbaccalaureate or graduate students. These students earned degrees outside of UPS and most likely used community colleges to refresh skills or complete prerequisites for graduate work.

## Implications for Community Colleges

As the reverse transfer population increases, community colleges are faced with the challenge to offer programs and courses that serve these students' academic and career goals. Several of the studies highlighted here provide useful insights for understanding reverse transfer students' needs. In the metropolitan area of Portland, Oregon, "students moved among the three community colleges and the university as if they were part of a single complex educational system despite the fact that the institutions are entities of four separate governments, with entirely separate financial processes and curriculum structures" (Kinnick and others, 1997, p. 8). If students consider disparate institutions to be part of a unified system of higher education, then community colleges need to remain flexible by easing the transferability of credits between institutions, providing innovative courses that pertain to the ever-changing workforce, and permitting students to enter and reenter as they please.

Another conception of the higher education system is offered by the Canadian students in Vaala's (1991) study: "Students attending a [two-year] college after a university do not see the postsecondary system in terms of 'feeder' and 'receiver' institutions. The students are more likely to see themselves as the client of one institution at a time" (p. 18). Therefore, community college administrators need to recognize that many of these students are focused on specific programs and training opportunities, not the transfer function.

Community college programs that serve reverse transfer students tend to help facilitate a positive environment for academic advancement. Kingsborough Community College's (KCC) New Start Program provided the opportunity for thousands of former four-year, prebaccalaureate students to demonstrate that they can succeed and earn degrees. Students entered this program after experiencing financial hardship, academic difficulty, or dissatisfaction with their four-year institutions. Through New Start, they are provided with specialized counseling and academic advisement. Because students' grades were not transferred from their four-year institutions, New Start applicants were admitted to KCC as matriculates in good academic standing. The success of these reverse transfer students is evident in the enrollment, graduation, and transfer rates. By March 1993, the program had enrolled 2,252 students. Nearly 23 percent had graduated from KCC, 13 percent had transferred to a four-year institution, and 27 percent had enrolled at KCC for the following term (Winchell and Schwartz, 1993).

## Implications for Future Research

Although McCormick and Carroll (1997) used data from a national sample to document some trends among reverse transfer students, they acknowledge that systematic analysis of student transfer from four-year to two-year institutions on a national scale is lacking. One possible reason for this paucity in the literature is the difficulty of tracking students whose enrollment patterns are contrary to the linear, vertical progression of the traditional educational pipeline. To remedy this situation, community college researchers and administrators need to recognize reverse transfer patterns as a unique aspect of the transfer function. More specifically, researchers and policymakers concerned with the transfer function must devote attention to the unique needs of reverse transfer students. This *phenomenon*—the term often used in the literature to describe reverse transfer patterns—shows no signs of disappearing; rather, it may reinforce the conception of community colleges as the bastion of lifelong learning.

The materials reviewed in this chapter reflect the most recent literature available in the ERIC database on reverse transfer students. Most ERIC documents (publications with ED numbers) can be viewed on microfiche at approximately nine hundred libraries worldwide. In addition, most may be ordered on microfiche or on paper copy from the ERIC Document Reproduction Services (EDRS) at (800) 443-ERIC. Journal articles may be acquired through regular library channels or purchased from one of the following article reproduction services: Carl Uncover [http://www.carl.org/uncover/], [uncover@carl.org] (800) 787-7979, UMI [orders@infostore.com] (800) 248-0360, or ISI [tga@isinet.com] (800) 523-1850.

## References

Baratta, F. *Profile of District Transfers to the University of California, California State University and St. Mary's College.* Martinez, Calif.: Contra Costa Community College District, 1992. (ED 349 066)

Bers, T. H. "Yet Another Look at Transfer: Oakton Students and Bachelor's Degree Recipients at Illinois Public Universities." Des Plaines, Ill.: Oakton Community College Office of Institutional Research, 1992. (ED 352 087)

Chan, C.-R., and McIntyre, C. "California Community College Report on Enrollment, 1993–94." Sacramento: California Community Colleges, Office of the Chancellor, 1995. (ED 377 927)

Kajstura, A., and Keim, M. C. "Reverse Transfer Students in Illinois Community Colleges." *Community College Review,* 1992, 20 (2), 39–44. (EJ 456 257)

Kinnick, M. K., Ricks, M. F., Bach, S., Walleri, D., Stoering, J., and Tapang, B. "Student Transfer and Outcomes Between Community Colleges and a University Within an Urban Environment." Annual forum paper. Orlando: Association for Institutional Research, 1997. (ED 410 895)

McCormick, A. C., and Carroll, D. C. "Transfer Behavior Among Beginning Postsecondary Students: 1989–94." Postsecondary Education Descriptive Analysis Reports. Statistical Analysis Report. Berkeley: MPR Associates, 1997. (ED 408 929)

Oklahoma State Regents for Higher Education, Oklahoma City. "Student Transfer Matrix, Fall 1996." Oklahoma City: Oklahoma State Regents for Higher Education, 1997. (ED 416 799)

Trombley, W. H. "Public Policy by Anecdote: The Case of Community College Fees." San Jose: California Higher Education Policy Center, 1993. (ED 356 806)

Vaala, L. "Attending Two-Year College After Attending a Four-Year University in Alberta, Canada." *Community College Review,* 1991, 18 (4), 13–20. (EJ 428 973)

Winchell, A., and Schwartz, C. P. "New Start Program 1993: Eighth-Year Report." Brooklyn, N.Y.: Kingsborough Community College, 1993. (ED 366 380)

*CHRISTINE M. LEBARD is a doctoral student in the Graduate School of Education and Information Studies, University of California, Los Angeles, and acquisitions-outreach assistant for the ERIC Clearinghouse for Community Colleges.*

# INDEX

# Back Issue/Subscription Order Form

Copy or detach and send to:
**Jossey-Bass Inc., Publishers, 350 Sansome Street, San Francisco, CA 94104-1342**

Call or fax toll free!
**Phone 888-378-2537 6AM-5PM PST; Fax 800-605-2665**

Back issues:    Please send me the following issues at $25 each
(Important: please include series initials and issue number, such as CC90)

1. CC _____

_____

_____

$ _____ Total for single issues

$ _____ Shipping charges (for single issues *only;* subscriptions are exempt
from shipping charges): Up to $30, add $5$^{50}$ • $30$^{01}$–$50, add $6$^{50}$
$50$^{01}$–$75, add $7$^{50}$ • $75$^{01}$–$100, add $9 • $100$^{01}$–$150, add $10
Over $150, call for shipping charge

Subscriptions    Please ❑ start  ❑ renew my subscription to *New Directions
for Community Colleges* for the year 19___ at the following rate:

❑ Individual $60    ❑ Institutional $107
**NOTE:** Subscriptions are quarterly, and are for the calendar year only.
Subscriptions begin with the spring issue of the year indicated above.
For shipping outside the U.S., please add $25.

$ _____ Total single issues and subscriptions (CA, IN, NJ, NY and DC
residents, add sales tax for single issues. NY and DC residents must
include shipping charges when calculating sales tax. NY and Canadian
residents only, add sales tax for subscriptions)

❑ Payment enclosed (U.S. check or money order only)

❑ VISA, MC, AmEx, Discover Card #_____ Exp. date_____

Signature _____ Day phone _____

❑ Bill me (U.S. institutional orders only. Purchase order required.)

Purchase order #_____

Name _____

Address _____

_____

_____

Phone_____ E-mail _____

For more information about Jossey-Bass Publishers, visit our Web site at:
www.josseybass.com    **PRIORITY CODE = ND1**

OTHER TITLES AVAILABLE IN THE
NEW DIRECTIONS FOR COMMUNITY COLLEGES SERIES
*Arthur M. Cohen*, Editor-in-Chief
*Florence B. Brawer*, Associate Editor